Praise for Practical Zendesk Administration

"In today's ever-changing business world, sustaining your competitive advantage comes down to maintaining great customer relationships. The Zendesk customer service platform has helped Box provide outstanding customer service, and the best practices in this book are a useful tool to help your organization do the same thing."

— *Aaron Levie*
Co-Founder and CEO at Box

"I can think of none more qualified to write this book than Stafford Vaughan. Not only is he an expert in Zendesk best practices, but his hands-on experience in using Zendesk and teaching Zendesk training courses means you'll learn valuable tips that will save you time and eliminate error. No Zendesk administrator should be without this book."

— *Micah Solomon*
Bestselling Author of *High-Tech, High-Touch Customer Service*

"Cloud, mobile and SaaS are driving radical changes in technology business models. Customer support models and expectations have changed too, and you need to be ready. Stafford has led hundreds of top companies to successful next-generation customer support. You won't find a greater expert on practices and approaches for Zendesk-driven customer support. If you're responsible for a Zendesk deployment, get this book now."

— *Carson Sweet*
Co-Founder and CEO at CloudPassage

"This book comes at the right point in time. We have already been using Zendesk for more than a year and a half, and feel we have a very good knowledge of the system, but this book provides additional hints and fresh insights into the system that have been really helpful. Due to the rapid evolution of Zendesk, such a book is ideal for beginners as well as old-timers."

— *Axel Focht*
Head of Customer Service at Groupon UK, IRL & DK

SECOND EDITION

Practical Zendesk Administration

Stafford Vaughan and Anton de Young

Beijing · Cambridge · Farnham · Köln · Sebastopol · Tokyo

Practical Zendesk Administration, Second Edition

by Stafford Vaughan and Anton de Young

Printed in the United States of America.

Published by O'Reilly Media, Inc., 1005 Gravenstein Highway North, Sebastopol, CA 95472.

O'Reilly books may be purchased for educational, business, or sales promotional use. Online editions are also available for most titles (*http://my.safaribooksonline.com*). For more information, contact our corporate/institutional sales department: 800-998-9938 or *corporate@oreilly.com*.

Editors: Mike Loukides and Andy Oram	**Cover Designer:** Randy Comer
Production Editor: Nicole Shelby	**Interior Designer:** David Futato
Copyeditor: Jasmine Kwityn	**Illustrator:** Rebecca Demarest
Proofreader: Rachel Monaghan	

October 2012:   First Edition

May 2014:   Second Edition

Revision History for the Second Edition:

2014-05-09:   First release

See *http://oreilly.com/catalog/errata.csp?isbn=9781491900697* for release details.

ISBN: 978-1-491-90069-7

[LSI]

This book is dedicated to Zendesk's founders—Mikkel Svane, Morten Primdahl, and Alexander Aghassipour—for dreaming up and building a simple yet powerful customer service platform. It has been our pleasure to teach people how to best use Zendesk for successfully providing support to their coworkers and customers around the world.

Table of Contents

Foreword

We built Zendesk back in 2007 because we were frustrated with the quality of the customer service applications that existed at the time. The vast majority of these "solutions" were big, clunky, on-premise enterprise applications, were distributed on CDs, and took forever to deploy. Even proof-of-concept projects often took months to complete. And when all was said and done, no one, especially the customer, was ever really satisfied.

Zendesk was the first truly cloud-based customer service application that you could sign up for, subscribe to, and configure online. Launching the application within an organization took hours instead of months.

Nowadays, it's hard to imagine software being distributed or packaged any other way. We helped revolutionize an entire industry in only five years, yet that handful of years seems like a lifetime ago. The changes in technology have been only part of the story. More important are the cultural shifts that the technology enabled, the changes in the very relationships between companies and their customers. The explosion of online social networks, crowd-sourced review sites, and subscription-based business models creates incredible opportunities (or challenges, depending on your perspective) for those businesses willing to shift their thinking about customer relationships. Our goal at Zendesk was always to help businesses realize those opportunities.

This manual—while it focuses on teaching administrators and agents how to use Zendesk better—can also set the groundwork for building better, simpler, more human customer relationships within your own organization. By learning how best to use Zendesk, you can accomplish larger organizational goals and changes: empowering employees to fully help customers, increasing responsiveness, becoming more transparent, and seeing and relating to your customers more fully.

We applaud any business that sets its sights beyond simple brand loyalty, and instead makes the shift toward customer relationships. It takes a ton of work, but it's worth it.

We couldn't ask for better guides into Zendesk than Stafford and Anton. Stafford created the original Zendesk training program and has helped hundreds of businesses use Zendesk to transform their own customer service operations. Anton has run the documentation team at Zendesk for three years, took over customer training in 2013, and knows the product inside and out. Aside from their deep product knowledge, both of them are gifted with the skill of making even the most complicated concepts seem simple, and they remain keenly focused on what is actually important: using Zendesk to accomplish your organization's goals.

Reading these chapters is like reading the advanced manual we never wrote when we designed the product. Stafford and Anton's ability to enlighten readers on how to use the product better and the reasons for the design decisions in Zendesk never ceases to impress us.

Passion is what drove Zendesk's founders to build the product before you today. But it is the success of our customers that built our company. More than 40,000 organizations around the world rely on Zendesk for great customer service and engagement. We believe this book can help all Zendesk admins and agents improve customer service and build better customer relationships for their organizations.

Happy reading! And if you are ever in San Francisco, let us know so we can buy you a drink.

—Mikkel Svane
Founder and CEO of Zendesk

Preface

In 2011, a survey was conducted to find out what people really value about the companies and brands they use. It may surprise you to know that when choosing among product quality, price, or customer service, 55% of people selected customer service as the most important factor in determining whether they would recommend a company.

The example I often give is this: imagine your friend has bought a pen. Now imagine you want to buy a pen for yourself, and you ask your friend whether she likes the pen she purchased. Statistically speaking, your friend is unlikely to say, "it's a good pen because it writes really well." She also won't say, "I like this pen because I got it for a good price" or "I like it because it doesn't smudge." No, statistically speaking, your friend is most likely to say, "I like this pen because, on the day it ran out of ink and I called the pen company, the customer service rep made me feel really good about owning this pen."

That is the sort of relationship Zendesk helps you achieve with your customers. For more details on this statistic, see the "Why Companies Should Invest in the Customer Experience" infographic (*http://bit.ly/customerex*).

The best way to describe this book is "the Zendesk consultant in book form." The advice, best practices, and pitfalls included in this book are the result of working in the trenches, launching Zendesk customer implementations, delivering training sessions, and answering literally thousands of questions from training participants in countries all over the world. Every question from a Zendesk training participant gives me a fresh perspective on new ways to use the product, which I've tried to capture and share in this book.

Zendesk is a popular customer service software tool, and its approach has always been to deliver a powerful solution with beautifully simple design. However, Zendesk's simple design philosophy should not lead you to believe that the product is not powerful. In fact, the entire purpose of this book is to bring the expansive set of Zendesk features to light, explain their purpose, demystify the best approach to use them, and help you to get the most out of the product.

In explaining the features of the Zendesk product, we've focused on best practices instead of the step-by-step configuration tasks carried out by an administrator. If you are completely new to Zendesk and you find that you're having trouble understanding some of the concepts in this book, we recommend taking a look at the official Zendesk user guide (*http://bit.ly/zendesk-usr*) before diving further into this book. This will ensure that you have a solid understanding of the features before getting the advice on best practices contained in this book. It may also help to build a strong foundation for the process of making important decisions about your Zendesk instance.

It's also worth noting that this book focuses specifically on best practices for the Zendesk product without going into depth on the broader techniques for providing outstanding customer service. Zendesk is a tool that can be wielded in any way that works best for your organization.

In his book *High-Tech, High-Touch Customer Service* (AMACOM, 2012), Micah Solomon describes the idea of "touching" customers as the starting point to developing a lasting relationship. It's impossible to physically touch customers over the Internet, but it's possible to use Zendesk to reach out to those customers and deliver that metaphorical touch. This book will get you to the point of using the tool to its full potential —all that's left is for you to use it. As Micah Solomon says, "the goal in all this is to touch customers in a way that builds true customer loyalty."

—Stafford Vaughan

Chapter Overviews

Chapter 1, Introduction to Zendesk
> Before diving into the Zendesk product itself, this chapter explains the most important concepts of the tool. By the end of this chapter, you'll understand many of the terms used in the product and the benefits of implementing Zendesk as your customer service solution.

Chapter 2, Initial Setup
> There is a small set of tasks that all Zendesk administrators should perform on their instances before allowing users to sign in. This chapter explains these initial setup tasks and focuses on the steps necessary to give your Zendesk environment the same branding as the rest of your organization. It also provides details on setting up your Zendesk instance for an international audience.

Chapter 3, Security
> Any website that captures personal information must be secure, and this chapter will help you to make decisions on the various security options in Zendesk.

Chapter 4, User Management

This chapter explains the various types of users that can be created (end users, agents, and administrators) and the roles of each one, as well as the different permissions you can configure for them.

Chapter 5, Channels

Zendesk is a tool that leverages many different methods of creating tickets, from common systems such as email to the newer approach of using social media platforms such as Facebook and Twitter. This chapter explains each of these channels, how to set them up, the benefits of each one, and how to make the most of them.

Chapter 6, Fields and Data Capture

Out of the box, Zendesk has a number of default fields that capture the standard information required by any customer service team. As an administrator, you have some control over these fields, as well as the ability to add new fields to your Zendesk instance.

Chapter 7, Agent Support Process

Making a support agent's life easier is a good idea for everyone involved. This chapter explains some of the techniques you can use to make the support process more efficient, as well as the best ways to manage the decisions that agents make on a daily basis.

Chapter 8, Automated Business Rules

Automating your business process in Zendesk will not only save your team time, it will also reduce the risk of mistakes. This chapter describes the various Zendesk features—including triggers and automations—you can use to achieve this. It also provides examples of common business processes and their associated business rules, which gives you an inside look into how other customer service teams operate.

Chapter 9, Help Center

The Zendesk Help Center allows you to provide self-service support to your customers. This chapter explains how to set up your Help Center and customize it to reflect your company's or organization's brand. This chapter also includes information on how to measure the use of your Help Center and constantly improve it.

Zendesk Version

The version of Zendesk covered in this book is the latest public release as of March 2014. Zendesk has a frequent—often weekly—release schedule, with new features and updates to existing features. The release notes are made available to the public in the official Release Notes forum (*http://bit.ly/release-note*). Throughout this book we've deliberately described features without giving detailed steps to configure them, and we've included screenshots only in situations when we believe that the explanation would not be complete without them. The purpose of this book is to focus on the advice and best practices for administering the product, rather than be a step-by-step guide. If you would like or need more detailed instructions, the official Zendesk user guides (*http://bit.ly/zendesk-usr*) may be a useful accompaniment to this book.

Conventions Used in This Book

The following typographical conventions are used in this book:

Italic
> Indicates new terms, URLs, email addresses, filenames, and file extensions.

`Constant width`
> Used for program listings, as well as within paragraphs to refer to program elements such as variable or function names, databases, data types, environment variables, statements, and keywords.

 This element signifies a tip, suggestion, or general note.

 This element indicates a warning or caution.

Safari® Books Online

 *Safari Books Online* is an on-demand digital library that delivers expert content in both book and video form from the world's leading authors in technology and business.

Technology professionals, software developers, web designers, and business and creative professionals use Safari Books Online as their primary resource for research, problem solving, learning, and certification training.

Safari Books Online offers a range of product mixes and pricing programs for organizations, government agencies, and individuals. Subscribers have access to thousands of books, training videos, and prepublication manuscripts in one fully searchable database from publishers like O'Reilly Media, Prentice Hall Professional, Addison-Wesley Professional, Microsoft Press, Sams, Que, Peachpit Press, Focal Press, Cisco Press, John Wiley & Sons, Syngress, Morgan Kaufmann, IBM Redbooks, Packt, Adobe Press, FT Press, Apress, Manning, New Riders, McGraw-Hill, Jones & Bartlett, Course Technology, and dozens more. For more information about Safari Books Online, please visit us online.

How to Contact Us

Please address comments and questions concerning this book to the publisher:

O'Reilly Media, Inc.
1005 Gravenstein Highway North
Sebastopol, CA 95472
800-998-9938 (in the United States or Canada)
707-829-0515 (international or local)
707-829-0104 (fax)

We have a web page for this book, where we list errata, examples, and any additional information. You can access this page at *http://bit.ly/zendesk-2e*.

To comment or ask technical questions about this book, send email to *bookques tions@oreilly.com*.

For more information about our books, courses, conferences, and news, see our website at *http://www.oreilly.com*.

Find us on Facebook: *http://facebook.com/oreilly*

Follow us on Twitter: *http://twitter.com/oreillymedia*

Watch us on YouTube: *http://www.youtube.com/oreillymedia*

Content Updates

This update to Practical Zendesk Administration brings all of the content up to date with the version of Zendesk that is available as of March 2014. The many user interface and workflow enhancements and new features added since the first version of the book was published have been added. The biggest change is that the new version of the Zendesk customer-facing support portal, Help Center, has replaced the older version, Web Portal, which was included in the first version of the book but is no longer available to new Zendesk customers. Many of the sections of the book have been updated as a result and a new chapter on Help Center replaced the previous Web Portal chapter, which was called "Forums". The other new Zendesk features that were added include the following:

- New security features:
  - Digitally Signed Outbound Email Communication
  - Administrative Audit Log

— Agent Device Management

- Customer Lists
- Multiple Organizations
- Support Email Addresses
- On-hold Ticket Status
- Custom User and Organization Fields
- Ticket Forms
- Markdown and Emoji support in ticket comments

CHAPTER 1

Introduction to Zendesk

Zendesk is a customer service solution that is designed to be beautifully simple, and is used by many of the world's largest organizations to provide support to their customers. It's a Software-as-a-Service (SaaS) product, which means that your organization will pay a monthly fee for every registered member of your support team using the product. Zendesk will take care of the hosting for you, as well as the other logistics of running a complex website, which allows you to focus on the important tasks—such as providing great support to your customers.

In this book we use the phrase *Zendesk instance*, which refers to the Zendesk environment of your organization, and presumably the environment you'll be administering. Unless your organization is very large, you will typically have one Zendesk instance. The domain name of the instance will be something like *mycompany.zendesk.com*. That is one Zendesk instance, and all of the settings discussed in this book can be applied to that instance.

Explanation of the Zendesk Plans

There are five different Zendesk plans, the features of which will be applied to your entire Zendesk instance:

Starter
> The name of this plan suggests that it's well suited to customers just getting started with Zendesk, which is true, but it's also a great fit for smaller shops with limited customization needs for the product. The total cost for this plan is $1/month for each agent (if billed annually) or $2/month for each agent (if billed monthly). It allows for up to three agent accounts. The best part is that a very deserving nonprofit organization gets a donation equal to your first year's subscription. Donations from the Starter plan have benefited the UCSF Benioff Children's Hospital and chari-

ty:water (a nonprofit organization that brings clean and safe drinking water to people in developing nations).

Regular

The Regular plan is designed for customers that don't need the bells and whistles of the higher plans. The cost for this plan is $25/month for each agent (if billed annually) or $29/month for each agent (if billed monthly). Unlike the Starter plan, there is no limit on the number of agents that can be included on this plan. The Regular plan is particularly well suited to customers who are satisfied with basic reporting functionality, and who are running Zendesk for customers in a single language and time zone. The support offered by Zendesk on this plan is limited to email support only.

Plus

This is the most popular option, and is the perfect plan for midsize to large organizations. Features of this plan include advanced business analytics with GoodData, as well as complete internationalization features and a number of tools to improve team collaboration. The cost of this plan is $59/month for each agent (if billed annually) or $69/month for each agent (if billed monthly). Similar to the Regular plan, there is no restriction on the number of agents that can be included on this plan. We highly recommend this plan to customers, and it provides the added benefit of both email and phone support from Zendesk.

Enterprise

For larger organizations, the Enterprise plan adds further security and compliance features, as well as the ability to maintain multiple connected Zendesk instances with separate branding for each. These features will not be necessary for everyone. On the other hand, a feature that is available only on the Enterprise plan—agent roles—is one of the most useful pieces of the entire product (see "Enterprise Agent Roles and Light Agents" on page 42 for further details). This feature alone can be worth the extra cost for some customers. I recommend that all Zendesk customers take a second glance at this plan (don't be scared by the "Enterprise" label, because it's something of a misnomer). The Enterprise plan is $125/month for each agent (if billed annually) or $139/month for each agent (if billed monthly), but when you consider that Light Agents are free accounts, it doesn't necessarily have to be more expensive than the other plans. As a bonus, this plan offers 24/7 support from the Zendesk support team.

Enterprise Elite

This plan is for large organizations who need or appreciate a higher level of support that is catered specifically to their needs. Elite customers receive support from a dedicated Zendesk Customer Success Manager who provides on-boarding assistance, special training, and regular check-ins, and advises on technical best practices, beta news, and opportunities to participate in by-invitation-only customer advisory events. This plan is available to Zendesk customers who purchase a contract of $100,000 or more per year.

For further information about the set of plans and the features contained in each one, visit the plan comparison page (*http://www.zendesk.com/compare*). Throughout this book we specifically state if a feature is available only on one of the more expensive plans. It's up to you to decide whether such features are necessary for your use case.

 Once you select a plan, all of the agents in the system will be on that plan. It's not possible to pick and choose plan features to delegate to certain agents in the system. If you have 100 agents on the Regular plan and you'd like to upgrade to the Plus plan, the additional cost will be for every agent currently enabled in the system.

Terms and Definitions

Rather than explaining all of the product terms up front, we'll explain only the most important concepts here. We'll wait until the individual chapters to introduce the terms more comprehensively. The following terms are so fundamental to Zendesk that many of the topics in this book won't make sense until you understand them:

Ticket
A support request submitted by a customer to ask for assistance. The term is selected to be as generic as possible, to capture the broad range of requests submitted to your customer service team.

Field
Before a ticket is submitted, the user will provide details about her request by entering values into the ticket fields. Examples of default *system fields* are Subject, Description, and Priority. It's also possible for administrators to add *custom fields*, which capture more specific information in the ticket.

Comment
These are pieces of text that are added to a ticket and form the conversation that will help solve it. Comments can be *public*, which means that they're visible to end users who have access to the ticket. Comments can also be *private*, which means that only members of your internal support team and administrators will be able to read them.

User
A user is anyone with an account in the Zendesk instance. All users are classified as one of three types: end users, agents, and administrators.

End user

An end user account is usually one that has been created by a customer when he submits a ticket. End users typically have access to their own tickets and sometimes tickets requested by other people at their organization, but never tickets requested by other user accounts. End users are also restricted as to the fields that they can view or edit, unless an administrator has enabled access to those fields.

Agent

An agent is typically a person who works for the support organization, providing assistance to customers. Agent access to tickets will vary according to permissions set up by administrators, but agents can typically access a wide range of tickets submitted by customers.

Administrator

Administrators are the users who have complete access to the Zendesk instance. They can control all settings and are able to read all tickets reported by all users. Administrator users are also classified as agents in the system, meaning that their access includes all of the agent functions, and that every administrator user is billed by Zendesk as an agent account. For the purposes of this book, we're assuming that you'll have full administrative privileges in your Zendesk instance.

Group

Groups are used to collect your agents together for the purpose of applying business rules or restricting visibility of a Zendesk feature. Groups can contain only agent or administrator accounts and cannot contain end users. Tickets in your Zendesk instance may be assigned to groups, which indicates the team of agents who are currently working on the ticket.

Organization

To collect your end users, you use organizations. Doing so allows you to apply different support processes to different sets of customers. For example, you're able to automatically assign a ticket from a user in a specific organization (from a specific company) to the agent group that provides support to that company.

Assignee

When an individual member of your support team is working on a ticket, she will be set as the assignee of a ticket. The assignee of a ticket must always be an agent, although in rare circumstances the assignee may be an administrator. This is because administrators typically set up and manage Zendesk instances but are not involved in solving tickets. But there's nothing preventing administrators from doing so, of course.

Requester

The person who is seeking assistance on the specific ticket. Requesters are typically end users, and will receive email notifications when the ticket is updated.

Channel

There are nine different ways for customers to create a ticket in Zendesk, and these are referred to as channels. The options include the Help Center, email, chat, phone, the Feedback Tab, Facebook, Twitter, ticket sharing, and the API. The various channels are one of the great advantages of Zendesk, because allowing customers to contact your support team using the method in which they're most comfortable is the first step to creating a positive customer service experience.

Views

Part of the agent business process will involve checking a specific list of tickets every day to find tickets to work on. Views are configurable saved searches that make it possible for agents to repeatedly find tickets according to the same criteria. Zendesk starts with a number of default views, but as an administrator, you can add new views according to the specific business process of your organization. Agents can also create personal views that only they can see.

Macros

When your agents solve tickets, they'll probably find that the same processes or questions are often repeated. Agents and administrators are able to create macros that capture a specific set of actions and store them in the form of a shortcut. The use of macros can save agents considerable time when solving support requests.

Help Center

Your customer-facing support portal is the Help Center, which includes both the Knowledge Base and the Community. It's where your customers go to find answers, participate in your community, request support, and track the support requests that they've already created. It's a separate application in your Zendesk instance, meaning that it exists in a separate browser window from the agent and administrator part of your Zendesk instance. The design is based on themes and is easily customizable so that you can change it to match your branding.

Knowledge Base

The Knowledge Base, one half of the customer-facing Help Center, is designed to support a self-service customer workflow by anticipating requests from customers and providing articles that answer these questions in advance. Providing a knowledge base for your customers may be one of the best first steps you can take when setting up Zendesk to provide support. A question answered via a search of your knowledge base means one fewer ticket in your queue or one fewer phone call for your agents. Research clearly indicates that customers prefer to find answers themselves.

Community

The other half of the Help Center is Community. If you're familiar with sites such as Stack Overflow, you already have some idea of what the Community feature in Help Center provides. Your customers can post questions into discussion topics (e.g., a topic about a specific product), and members of your user community provide answers. The best or correct answer is marked as such and moved to the top of the answer thread. The Community feature in Help Center is an invaluable companion to your knowledge base and allows your customers to create their own discussion threads and to help each other learn and use your products and services.

Triggers

When tickets are created or updated, triggers will be fired to execute a specific set of actions. Typically the actions will include sending an email notification to users about the update, but other triggers might be used to change a field on a ticket according to certain criteria.

Automations

Automations are similar to triggers in that their function is to automatically execute a set of actions, but the difference is that automations will be executed after a certain amount of time passes. Typically automations are useful for setting reminders or defining escalations.

Email notifications

These are simply emails that are sent from Zendesk to your users. Zendesk uses email notifications to keep in touch with users in a number of contexts; for example, notifications will be sent when users are created or when knowledge base articles are added. They can also be configured in triggers and automations. The template for all of these email notifications is consistent, which will be explained later in this book.

Business process

Generally we use the term *business process* to refer to a process that is followed or defined by your organization. The business processes of organizations are usually what makes them so unique. Some processes are less tangible, and will involve a set of instructions being provided to your support agents. Other processes can be defined in Zendesk more tangibly, and when this happens, they are termed *business rules*.

Business rules

These are the automated processes that are defined in Zendesk. Business rules can be agent rules (such as views and macros) or global rules (such as triggers and automations). Other rules can also be configured through the administrator interface of Zendesk.

User Interface Experience

The Zendesk user interface is separated into three distinct experiences, each representing one of the types of user profiles (i.e., end users, agents, and administrators).

After signing in as an administrator, you can open the product administration section directly by clicking the Admin icon in the lower-left corner of every screen. This icon looks like a cog, and is visible in Figure 1-1. Once inside the administration console, you will see a list of the administration menu options, grouped by category, on the lefthand side of the screen. After opening one of the administration menu items, you'll see the options for that section of the product on the righthand side of the menu. Figure 1-1 shows an example of the Zendesk administration screen. The toolbar appears on the lefthand side of the screen, the administration navigation is beside it, and the Apps Marketplace page occupies the rest of the screen.

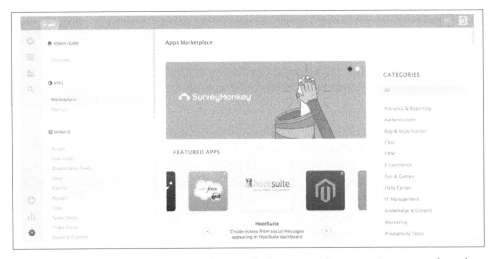

Figure 1-1. Administrator user interface, with the Apps administration page selected

When agents are signed in to Zendesk, they have a slightly different experience than administrators. Their experience is focused on the toolbar icons in the upper left, including the buttons to view a list of tickets or to create new tickets. The end user experience also differs because end users only use the Help Center.

Examples of the ticket screens from the agent and end user interfaces are shown in the section "Data Capture Lifecycle" on page 85.

Administrators can use the "Assume identity" feature (explained in more detail on page 51) to sign in as an end user and see what that user sees in her view of the Help Center. This can be very useful in troubleshooting issues end users may have when using the Help Center.

Most of the user interface design elements in Zendesk use standard conventions, with a tendency on the side of simplicity. There are two unconventional design elements worth mentioning:

Deleting items

In some software products, when you see a list of items, a Delete button will often appear beside the item that you want to delete. This allows you to delete the item from a list directly. However, in Zendesk, this Delete button is hidden on the Edit page, so you'll first need to click the Edit link for the item (a macro, for example), then click the Delete button (located beside the button to submit the form). You can also delete a ticket through the Delete command in the "Ticket options" menu of a ticket. However, while it might be common practice to make it easy to delete information, it's not really best practice—especially when it comes to tickets. Maintaining the historical integrity of items such as tickets is important in customer service tools, and you really should only delete a ticket if it is junk (not a real support issue from a real customer that needs to be solved).

Secondary hover operations

When you read a list of items in Zendesk, the edit operation will usually be available via an Edit link on the far right column of the list. If you hover your mouse over an item in the list, you may also notice some secondary operations visible only when you're hovering. The most common example is the Deactivate link, which is a hover operation, or the Clone function, which is also visible only when hovering the mouse over an item in a list. To execute these operations, you'll need to hover the mouse over the item in the list and then click the link. There's no way to make these hover operations visible on the page permanently.

Steps to Administer Zendesk

There's no single set of steps that every Zendesk administrator must follow, and there is no specific order in which you must take the steps to configure your Zendesk instance successfully. Your Zendesk instance might leverage the default, out-of-the-box configuration with only minor changes before your agents sign in and get started. It's also possible that you'll change every one of the settings in the product or find ways to configure the product to do something new and creative, just because it suits the needs and processes of your organization.

We've tried to order the topics in this book in a logical sequence that works for most administrators. We recommend that you follow along with the topics in the order in which they are presented, and configure the product in the same order. By the time you've finished the book, you will have fully configured your Zendesk instance. This is not a requirement, though, and if you'd like to jump, say, to Chapter 5 because you're curious specifically about the topics in that chapter, that might work as well.

Internal Versus External Customer Service

Most of this book is dedicated to the idea that you'll be providing support to your customers. In the section "Terms and Definitions" on page 3, we defined end users as your customers, and your agents as your support staff. This is the most common usage of the product. It's not the only usage of the product, though. As a customer service tool, Zendesk can also be used internally within your organization. For example, it could be used by your IT Operations team to provide support to the rest of your organization. If you're using Zendesk in this way, you'll need to do some mental translations as you're reading this book. When we describe the "customers," we'll be referring to people at your organization who will be getting support. When we refer to your "support team," we're referring to the agents in Zendesk, who would be your IT Operations team in this example. In general, it doesn't hurt to still consider the team members at your organization as "customers," because in a way, anyone who submits a ticket deserves outstanding customer service from the team that is using Zendesk.

If you decide to use Zendesk to support a team internally within your organization, and all of the people at your organization are end users and your support team are the only agents in Zendesk, there's not really going to be a big difference from the standard use of the product. On the other hand, if you give your employees—who are the people submitting tickets—agent profiles in your Zendesk instance (instead of end-user profiles), there are a few configuration items that you might want to customize:

- The automated actions that move a ticket from the Pending or Solved statuses into Open (as described in "Ticket Status" on page 96) will not be fired if the email is from an agent account. The workaround will be that your business process should monitor updates to tickets on a regular basis.
- If the requester is forwarding an email and the Agent Forwarding feature (described on page 59) is enabled, the most recent comment on the email will be removed from the ticket. Zendesk will also request the ticket on behalf of someone else. To avoid this, you might want to consider disabling the Agent Forwarding feature.
- Agents cannot provide feedback using the Customer Satisfaction feature (described on page 151).

Many organizations run Zendesk very successfully as an internal customer service tool, but it is important to take these items under consideration to determine how they will impact your particular Zendesk instance.

Common Customer Service Concepts

Many of the terms used by Zendesk (e.g., *agent* and *ticket*) are standard in the industry. If you've used customer service software before, these terms will be familiar to you, as will many of the other terms used in the product. Zendesk also has product-specific terms, some of which are explained in the "Terms and Definitions" on page 3, and some of which are explained throughout this book.

If you're acquainted with the Information Technology Infrastructure Library (ITIL), which is a framework for how to deliver customer service, some of the features of Zendesk may already be familiar to you. For example, Zendesk uses the incident and problem relationship for convenient resolution of a large number of issues at once. Two of the three Zendesk founders are ITIL Foundation certified, and when they created Zendesk, they included many of the best practices from ITIL in the product. ITIL tends to be an extremely complex definition for how to deliver customer service, so you should be aware that Zendesk is a more simplified version of this.

CHAPTER 2

Initial Setup

Every Zendesk instance has a set of features that you'll need to configure once, and a set of features that you'll configure on an ongoing basis. This chapter deals primarily with the former, and covers most of the options that you'll choose during the very early phases of your implementation, and generally will not need to change afterward.

Some of the topics in this chapter—especially the email and domain name setup—may require assistance from teams other than your own, so it's best to get in early and configure these features now, even if you haven't fully defined your business process.

Creating a Sandbox

Before you start the configuration of any Zendesk environment, it's important to understand that for every Zendesk instance on the Plus or Enterprise plans, there is another instance known as a *sandbox*. In a nutshell, the sandbox is an environment for testing, learning, and making mistakes. We mention the sandbox at this point in the book because it's something that you'll probably want to use as you follow along with the topics in the book and start to configure your own environment. It's not possible to transfer the settings from your sandbox environment directly to your production environment, but after learning how to use each of the features covered in this book, you should find it fairly simple to repeat the configuration. I also find that it's best to complete your configuration in the sandbox environment and confirm that all features are working in conjunction with each other before starting the process of configuring your production environment.

To create a new sandbox as an administrator, select the "Create sandbox" administrative action. The first time you create a sandbox, you'll receive a confirmation message listing which settings will be copied and which will not (Figure 2-1). Zendesk copies some administrative settings, but not all of them. Most notably, it does not copy live ticket or user data. The general rule is that only low-impact settings are copied, such as your branding and channel options, to avoid messy mistakes with emailing live data to customers during testing. Also, all administrator users will be copied into the new sandbox with the same passwords as your production instance.

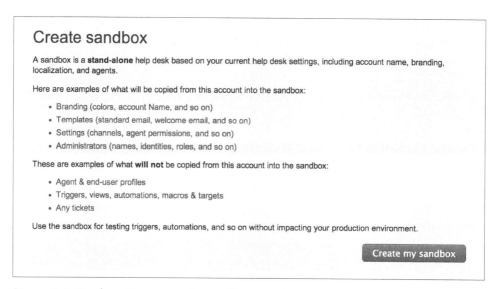

Create sandbox

A sandbox is a **stand-alone** help desk based on your current help desk settings, including account name, branding, localization, and agents.

Here are examples of what will be copied from this account into the sandbox:

- Branding (colors, account Name, and so on)
- Templates (standard email, welcome email, and so on)
- Settings (channels, agent permissions, and so on)
- Administrators (names, identities, roles, and so on)

These are examples of what **will not** be copied from this account into the sandbox:

- Agent & end-user profiles
- Triggers, views, automations, macros & targets
- Any tickets

Use the sandbox for testing triggers, automations, and so on without impacting your production environment.

Create my sandbox

Figure 2-1. Confirmation screen for sandbox creation

Your sandbox URL will be a unique web address based on your production environment URL. If your Zendesk instance is available at *<companyname>.zendesk.com*, the sandbox URL will be something like *<companyname>1325888214.zendesk.com*. That URL includes a numerically incrementing number, unique to every sandbox created. Once it's been created, you can visit your sandbox by signing in to Zendesk and selecting the "Go to sandbox" administrative action.

The great thing about the sandbox is that if you mess everything up, it's very easy to create a new empty sandbox. To do this, simply open your production instance again and select the "Reset sandbox" administrative action. This will first delete the existing sandbox, then create an empty sandbox with a new URL, ready for more testing.

Help Center Branding

The Zendesk customer-facing support portal, called Help Center, is your customers' view of your Zendesk instance, where they can request support, use your knowledge base, and participate in your community. It's a separate application from the agent and administrator interface. The Help Center is the part of Zendesk that can be customized and branded; the agent and administrator interface cannot. This makes sense from Zendesk's perspective because agents and administrators work in the back office, so to speak, whereas your customers visit your support site expecting a user experience that appears to be a seamless extension of your website.

As an administrator, you can customize your Help Center, which is based on themes and provides an easy-to-use interface. You can make simple style changes using color pickers and font choosers, or more elaborate changes with Cascading Style Sheets (CSS) and JavaScript.

Help Center Customization Using CSS and JavaScript

If you're inclined and have the necessary skills, you can also use CSS and JavaScript technology to modify the end-user look and feel of your Help Center entirely. There are many examples of Zendesk instances with attractive interface customizations, including:

- School of Rock (*http://helpdesk.schoolofrock.com*)
- bettercloud (*http://support.bettercloud.com*)
- charity: water (*http://support.charitywater.org*)
- Rockstar Games (*http://support.rockstargames.com*)
- box (*http://support.box.com*)

CSS and JavaScript customization instructions are not covered in this book, but the Zendesk site has a useful post, "CSS Cookbook for Help Center," (*http://bit.ly/css-ckbk*) that provides all the details.

Customizing the Zendesk URL

The URL, or web address, of a new Zendesk instance will be based on the subdomain selected during the setup process. For example, if your company name is "Blue Skies," your Zendesk URL might be *blueskies.zendesk.com*. For the purposes of this example, let's assume that the company's main website is *blueskies.com*. Although Zendesk would love for all of its customers to have the word "zendesk" in their Help Center URL, most customers prefer to change this to hide the Zendesk name, in favor of their own company name in the URL. If you're on the Regular, Plus, or Enterprise plans, you will be able to customize this URL. Customers such as Box, charity:water, bettercloud, and Rockstar Games use a method of prefixing the company URL with the word *support*.

There are several benefits to customizing the URL of your Help Center:

Customer convenience
If you use a subdomain of your primary domain name (e.g., the Help Center sub-domain of *blueskies.com* would be *support.blueskies.com*), this makes it easier for

customers to predict the URL of your support site. Your customers are far more likely to visit the *support.blueskies.com* URL to get support from Blue Skies than to visit *blueskies.zendesk.com*, which would require them to have prior knowledge that the Blue Skies company uses Zendesk.

Portability

If, at a later date, you decide that you'd rather not continue to use Zendesk as your customer service tool, it's much more convenient and reliable for you to redirect the *support.blueskies.com* domain name to your new support portal than to communicate a new URL to all of your customers.

White labeling

Rather than publicize that they're using Zendesk as their support portal, some organizations prefer to white-label their use of Zendesk, meaning that the support portal looks similar to their website but doesn't use the word *Zendesk*. The benefit for the company is that it keeps a cohesive brand throughout the website, without the appearance of many technologies connected together. Fortunately, Zendesk is very good with its integrations, which allow you to fully customize the Help Center interface using CSS and JavaScript, and also integrate your user account with an internal database by using single sign-on (see "Integrating with an External User Database" on page 30 for further information).

Customization of your Zendesk URL involves two steps. The first step is to set up a *Canonical Name* (CNAME) record with your Domain Name Service (DNS) provider. The CNAME record is basically an alias for the URL prefix, which redirects the user to another location. If you choose the *support.* prefix, which is the most common, you would need to set up a CNAME record in your DNS to redirect "support" to the full URL of the Zendesk instance, which is *blueskies.zendesk.com* in my example. Making this specific change (along with the following step) would allow customers to visit the domain name *support.blueskies.com*, and it would load the same *blueskies.zendesk.com* Zendesk instance. From the customers' perspective, the domain name would always appear to be *support.blueskies.com*. If you do not have the experience or qualifications to make a DNS change yourself, you can ask a member of your IT team or service provider to do it for you.

After the CNAME record is set up, you'll need to wait between 2 and 48 hours, which is enough time for your settings to be propagated to all DNS servers in the world.

The second step is more simple, and is something that you can change inside Zendesk yourself. If you've set up your CNAME record correctly and the change has propagated, go to the Domain tab inside the Account administration page, and you'll find the "Host mapping" option at the top of the page. Continuing the preceding example, the value for the "Host mapping" field would be *support.blueskies.com*. If the changes and propagation were successful, Zendesk will accept the setting. Otherwise, you'll receive a message that the CNAME has not been set up properly, and you'll need to check your settings and wait longer.

 If you're on either the Plus or Enterprise plan and using SSL on your Zendesk instance—which is something that we strongly encourage you to do—you should make sure to read "Secure Sockets Layer (SSL)" on page 34. That section explains how to set up SSL on a custom domain name, which will ensure that Zendesk does not revert to the default URL when using a secure connection.

Once all of these changes have been made, you and your customers should be able to visit the new URL that you've chosen, and the word *zendesk* will never appear in the URL again.

Internationalization

At the time of writing, the Zendesk Help Center interface supports 38 different languages. The administrator and agent interfaces support the following 23 languages: Chinese (Simplified), Chinese (Traditional), Danish, Dutch, English (US), English (Canada), English (UK), French, French Canadian, German, Italian, Japanese, Korean, Norwegian, Polish, Portuguese, Brazilian Portuguese, Spanish, Latin American Spanish, Swedish, Russian, Turkish, and Ukrainian. For geographically dispersed users, Zendesk also supports every time zone in the world.

As Zendesk spreads to organizations throughout the world, much greater attention is being given to the internationalization needs of these customers. In the last several years, Zendesk added a translated agent interface, the ability to create text translations, and automatic language detection of incoming emails. Behind the scenes, Zendesk also has features that will check browser headers of Help Center visitors, which adjusts the visitor's language settings automatically. All of these features help you to ensure that a great customer support experience starts in the local language of visitors to your Help Center.

Administrator Interface Language

The Zendesk administrator interface supports the 23 languages listed in the previous section. To change your language selection, you'll need to click your profile picture in the upper-right corner of the screen and select the option to edit your profile. The profile page has a drop-down list with all of the supported languages in the product. After updating your selection you should refresh your browser window, and…voilà! Everything is in French. Or German. Or Italian. Or one of the 20 other options currently supported.

Zendesk is constantly adding new languages to the administrator and agent interfaces, so if you don't see your language, you can try asking the Zendesk support team when your language will be supported by the agent and administrator interfaces.

Setting the Time Zone

Accurate times and dates are important in every customer service tool, and Zendesk allows time zones to be adjusted on a global and individual user basis.

To change the global time zone of your Zendesk instance, open the Localization tab on the Account administration page, select the appropriate option from the list of available time zones, and then click "Save tab." Once set, all times and dates will be displayed to users relative to the time zone selected. This is an important change to make, because customer service is a timely activity by its nature, and a time that suggests the last update was eight hours ago, when it was really one hour ago, could cause a lot of customer confusion and anger. Setting the correct time zone for your instance avoids these problems.

If you're on either the Plus or Enterprise plan, Zendesk has a feature that will allow all users to set their own personal time zone. All new user profiles will use the time zone selected as the global setting by default, but individual agents and end users can adjust their own time zone by editing their profile and selecting the time zone from the list of options.

On the Localization tab on the Account administration page you can also to select between 24-hour (military) time and 12-hour time. The default is 24-hour time, and this setting will be applied to all users, regardless of their individual time zone selection. Unless you're literally *in the military*, I don't think there's a best practice associated with this feature; it's a subjective decision made by the administrators and imposed on all users.

Multilanguage Support for End Users

Administrators can enable or disable certain languages, depending on the location of their customer base, and they can also select a default language other than English for their instance. In general, we recommend enabling as many languages as you will *possibly* need, rather than including only those languages you're absolutely sure you will need. It doesn't cost anything to add a language, and there's very little additional overhead (an exception to this is covered in "Dynamic Content for Text Translation" on page 17). Most of the Zendesk user interface is translated automatically, so adding a fringe language might make only one more customer happy, but it will be nice to have that happy customer.

To get started with enabling languages other than English, open the Localization tab in the Account administration page. There is a drop-down list to choose the default language, and below that there is a link to display "Additional languages." The latter option is available only to users on the Plus or Enterprise plans. After opening the list of additional languages, you can use the checkboxes to select the languages in which you'd like to offer support to your customers. Once you've made your selections, click "Save tab."

As soon as you've enabled new languages using the technique just described, end users will see a drop-down menu in the Help Center, as shown in Figure 2-2, allowing them to switch to a different language. When the user selects a new language, all text that is a noneditable part of the Zendesk user interface will be automatically updated. Behind the scenes, Zendesk will also detect the location of visitors based on their computer and browser settings, and will attempt to automatically select an appropriate language for the user.

Figure 2-2. Selecting a language in the Help Center

Although all of the words in the Help Center user interface are translated by default, you'll need to have any content you add to your Help Center translated yourself. You start with an article in your default language (English, for example) and then create language-specific versions for the languages that you support in your Help Center. When Zendesk detects the user's language, the correct version of the article is shown. You can also set a separate name for your Help Center for every language you support.

All of the outgoing notifications to your customers can be configured to display relevant content in the language the user has selected, and these will all be explained later in this book.

Dynamic Content for Text Translation

Dynamic content is a feature that allows standard pieces of text to be defined and associated with a special code (known as a *placeholder*). Translated versions of the text will then be displayed to users who speak a language other than English. Dynamic content is most useful in email templates and macros, and is available only to users on the Plus or Enterprise plans.

You can easily enable multiple languages in your Zendesk instance and also customize the text in your email notifications, macros, automations and triggers, ticket forms, and ticket and user and organization fields. However, Zendesk does not automatically translate this content for you. For this reason, if you're using multiple languages in Zendesk, it's also very important that you take advantage of the dynamic content feature. From the customer's perspective, there's nothing worse than having been led to believe that one's language is fully supported and then receiving an email notification that is only in English. This situation can be avoided with dynamic content, which allows you to create those translated versions of text.

To get started, open the "Dynamic content" administration page. A brand new Zendesk instance will not have any pieces of dynamic content defined, but it's quite easy to define your own.

To explain dynamic content, we're going to use a simple example of writing a set of instructions to reset a forgotten password. We revisit this topic in "Referring Macros to the Knowledge Base" on page 128 to explain an even better practice for doing this, but let's start with the basics in this exercise.

After you've clicked "add item" on the main "Dynamic content" page, the first field on the configuration page will be the Name. The value in this field will be used as a reference in several places throughout the product, so it's important that you select something that is meaningful and descriptive. For this example, we'll call our piece of dynamic content "Forgotten Password Instructions." Next, set the default language to English. The default language is the one used when a translation has not been defined for the specific language selected by the end user. Finally, define the content. In our example, the content would be a series of steps for the user to change her password. An example of this process is shown in Figure 2-3. When you're finished, click Create, and you'll have your first piece of dynamic content.

Every translation of a piece of dynamic content is called a *variant*. It's best to define a variant for every language that you have enabled in your Zendesk instance; otherwise, users may end up seeing a default piece of text, which is probably in a language other than what they selected.

To add a new variant, click the "add variant" link, select the language, and enter the same instructions (in our example, the series of steps to change the password) translated into the specified language. Repeat this process for all languages to be supported, and your screen will look similar to Figure 2-4.

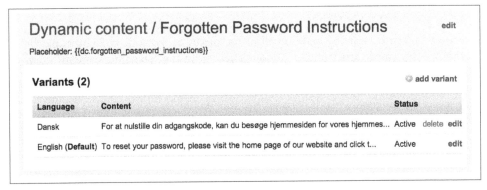

Dynamic content item title

Forgotten Password Instructions

Default language

English ▾

The default language of this dynamic content item.

Content

To reset your password, please visit the home page of our website and click the "I forgot my password" link. This page will ask you to enter your email address, and after you submit the form, we'll send you a link to reset your password.

The text of the dynamic content. You can also use placeholders in your text.

Cancel **Create**

Figure 2-3. Dynamic content creation screen

Dynamic content / Forgotten Password Instructions   edit

Placeholder: {{dc.forgotten_password_instructions}}

Variants (2)   ◉ add variant

Language	Content	Status		
Dansk	For at nulstille din adgangskode, kan du besøge hjemmesiden for vores hjemmes...	Active	delete	edit
English (**Default**)	To reset your password, please visit the home page of our website and click t...	Active		edit

Figure 2-4. Dynamic content summary screen, showing two variants

The key to using dynamic content is placeholders, which are explained in more detail on page 150. However, for the moment, suffice it to say that the automatically generated placeholder for our example is {{dc.forgotten_password_instructions}}. This is a special code used by Zendesk to refer to the piece of dynamic content. When I add this placeholder to an email or macro, it will be converted automatically to show text in the language selected by the user who will read the information. If the placeholder is used in an email template, the relevant user for the purposes of translation will be the recipient of the email. If the placeholder is used in a macro, the relevant user for the purposes of translation will be the requester of the ticket.

In the case of dynamic content on screen elements, the language selection will be based on the viewer of the text. In the case of dynamic content in emails, even if the agent executing a macro has selected English as his language, the variant selected for the dynamic content in the macro will be based on the requester's language selection.

There are many alternatives to using dynamic content, such as creating a different macro for every language in the system. I find that when it comes to text that needs to be translated, dynamic content is a bit more complex, but saves time and effort further down the track. It also decreases clutter in your Zendesk instance, and reduces the number of configurations required by administrators.

Bulk Translations

Instead of translating your dynamic content one piece at a time, you can define the standard pieces of dynamic content, then export the list and update all of the translations simultaneously. This makes the process of translating your entire Zendesk instance more scalable, and is particularly useful if you're using a translation agency, because you won't need to give it access to Zendesk.

To use this feature, start by defining all of the pieces of dynamic content using the technique described earlier in this section. Then, from the "Dynamic content" management page, click the "Export content" link on the right side of the screen. When you click the Export button, you'll see a message saying that the export is in progress, and you'll receive an email when it is complete. You should check your email inbox and follow the link to download the ZIP file of translations.

Every language supported by your Zendesk instance will have its own file contained inside the ZIP file. The format of each of these files is comma-separated values (CSV), with each row representing a piece of dynamic content to be translated. If you provide this file to a translation agency, it should send back the file in the same format, but the contents of the "X text" column should be updated to include the translated versions. The letter X must be replaced with the unique code for each language; for example, the Danish language code is "da" and the corresponding column is named "da text" in the CSV file.

The format of the CSV file is crucial when you're performing import operations. Common mistakes include opening the CSV file in Excel and then saving it as the wrong file format, or adding or renaming columns. If any of these changes occur, Zendesk will notify you that the file format is not valid when you try to import the translations file. It's possible for you to *remove* columns from the CSV file, so long as you keep the two mandatory columns: Title and "X text," where X is replaced with the language code. Generally, we recommend keeping all columns in the CSV file after exporting; otherwise, you introduce risk into the process. It's also very valuable to keep the "Default text" column in the CSV file, because it's a useful point of reference for the person translating the piece of text.

After translation, you'll need to import each of the CSV files into Zendesk individually. It's not possible to import all files as a ZIP file, and if you try, Zendesk will flag this as "Malformed CSV input." To start the import, select the "Import content" link from the same place as the link that exports content, then browse to the file and upload it. If your format is correct, your content will be updated immediately. If your format is incorrect, Zendesk will notify you via email.

Outgoing Email

Zendesk relies heavily on email for communication with users. When you originally create your Zendesk instance, the default email address will be set based on the subdomain name of your instance, but most customers prefer to customize the email address to be something more simple or consistent with their branding. This section will provide instructions on how to configure your outgoing emails, and how to ensure that security and spam controls are set up correctly. For an explanation of how to find the email templates used by outgoing emails in Zendesk, see "Email Notifications" on page 147.

Customizing the Email Domain

Continuing our example from earlier, if our Zendesk URL is *blueskies.zendesk.com*, Zendesk will automatically assign an email prefix of *support@* to our sender email address, producing a default support address of *support@blueskies.zendesk.com*. Again, this email address has the word *zendesk* in it, which may confuse many customers and should thus be avoided (for more on this, refer back to "Customizing the Zendesk URL" on page 13). The other benefit of removing the *zendesk* part from your incoming email address is that it's easier for customers to remember *support@blueskies.com* than *support@blueskies.zendesk.com* when emailing your support team.

Before changing the default support address of outgoing emails, you'll need to ensure that your mail server is configured to capture responses to the emails. Assuming that *support@blueskies.com* is the sender address of our emails, unless emails sent to *support@blueskies.com* are configured to make their way into our Zendesk instance, the responses will be lost in the ether.

In order to make this change, you'll need to ask your mail server administrators to forward to your Zendesk email address all incoming emails that are addressed to your designated support address. The exact method to do this varies depending on your mail service provider, but the process is usually common knowledge for mail server administrators, and a list of the steps for the popular services (Gmail, Yahoo! Mail, and Microsoft Exchange) is available in the Zendesk knowledge base article on the topic (*http://bit.ly/email-docs*). As long as your email administrators understand that the objective is for all emails sent to your instance's default support address (in this example, *support@blueskies.zendesk.com*) to be redirected to your main support email address (i.e., *support@blueskes.com*), they can make the change and it will be applied immediately.

Email Notification Sender Address

When a change occurs to a ticket in Zendesk, a feature called *triggers* generates an email notification to affected users. Other events—such as the creation of a user account—also generate an email notification to users. The email address used as the sender of these emails will vary, depending on the configuration options that you select in the "Email channel" administration page, and some other options for configuration are revisited in "Bidirectional Email Communication" on page 147.

The first step in changing the sender address is to open the Email section on the Channels administration page, and add a new support address. After you've made this change, outgoing emails will be sent from this address. It's usually best to allow your customers to reply directly to email notifications—which will add their response into Zendesk. Thus, the common convention of prefixing your email notifications with *noreply@* is not our recommended practice. Choosing an email address prefix such as *support@* is a good choice, because this will typically be the email address for your incoming email channel (covered on page 58).

Personalized Email Replies

By default, the sender name of email notifications will be the same as the name used in the default support address. Some customers find this to be a little bit impersonal—after all, the support experience should be with a real person and not an inanimate customer service tool.

To ensure the most personalized experience for your customers, Zendesk has a feature named *personalized email replies*. This very simple feature will change the sender name on outgoing emails to be the name of the agent who triggered the notification.

To explain this by example, if this feature is enabled and an agent named Erin replies to a support ticket saying, "Thanks for submitting this ticket, we'll send a response shortly," the name of the sender of the email will be "Erin" and the email address will be "*support@blueskies.com*."

This format also allows Zendesk to ensure that your primary Zendesk email address is not labeled in your address book as "Erin." Most email programs have a feature so that when you email somebody once, the recipient's details are saved in your address book. If the name "Erin" was associated with the address *support@blueskies.com* in your address book, it would be a problem because the next time you try to email Erin, you might email *support@blueskies.com* instead and reach the entire support team. The opposite can also be true—you might be trying to email the whole Blue Skies support team, but all you see in your address book is "Erin." For this simple reason, Zendesk uses the prefixed personalized email name for direct agent-to-customer communication and saves your default support address (e.g., *support@blueskies.com*) for system notifications not related to a specific ticket or agent.

Sender Policy Framework (SPF) Settings

The protocol used on the Internet to send email, known as SMTP, is defined so that anyone in the world could send an email pretending to be any other email address, and the email would still be sent. The catch is that most people have spam filters, and spam filters are clever at recognizing fake emails (known as "spoofed" emails). Spam filters can identify spoofed emails by checking the location of the sender of the email, and comparing that to the location of the company that the sender is pretending to be. If those locations differ, there is a high chance that the email will be identified as spam.

When Zendesk sends emails on behalf of your company, this situation occurs. Fortunately, you can fix it easily. If you've customized the domain name of the sender address for emails, it's very important that you also follow the steps in this section.

First, you'll need your DNS administrator to change the Sender Policy Framework, or SPF, rules for the relevant domain name. Essentially, this causes your domain name to tell the world that it trusts Zendesk to send emails on your behalf. Then, if a spam filter checks for validity, the email will not be flagged as spam. The specific SPF record to be added to most customer's DNS settings is `v=spf1 include:_spf.zdsys.com ?all`, and there are more detailed instructions in an article in the Zendesk knowledge base (*http://bit.ly/ext-email*).

> The SPF record for your specific mail configuration may vary depending on which service your company uses to host its domain name and which mail server you are using, although most domain name administrators should have the required knowledge to make this change.

Digitally Signed Outbound Email

If you're on the Plus or Enterprise plans, after you've customized the domain name of the sender address for emails, you can add another layer of protection against email spoofing by digitally signing your outbound email. This ensures that email sent from your Zendesk instance actually came from someone in your organization.

Zendesk supports DKIM (Domain Keys Identified Mail) and DMARC (Domain-based Message Authentication, Reporting & Conformance) authentication, and all email systems that support these protocols check inbound email to see if messages are properly digitally signed. If they are, those messages are delivered. If not, the message may be delivered with a caution or completely discarded.

Setting this up involves changes to the CNAME record of your external domain and may also require some help from your DNS administrator. Not all DNS providers support this feature, so you should check with your DNS administrator first. Zendesk has provided more detailed instructions in an article in the Zendesk knowledge base (*http://bit.ly/digi-sign*).

CHAPTER 3

Security

By its nature, customer service software captures personal information about people and organizations. This information is stored in the cloud as a SaaS solution. The idea of customer information being stored outside of a company's firewall often makes administrators nervous, but the reality is that any company in a position similar to Zendesk understands the potential security concerns, and takes every possible precaution to mitigate risk. Zendesk has some extraordinarily large companies in its customer list, and the security team takes the privacy of the information in your Zendesk instance very seriously.

The topics in this chapter will help you, as an administrator, to take best advantage of the security features in Zendesk.

Social Media Logins

As part of its integration with popular social media platforms, Zendesk has integrated its user management system in a way that allows users to sign in using these platforms (if this feature is enabled by an administrator). The benefit to your customers is that they do not need to memorize a dedicated username and password for Zendesk, because they're using a username and password that already exists in another system. From Zendesk's perspective, the tool is basically saying, "If you can successfully sign in to one of these social media platforms, we trust that platform enough to accept their word on the fact that you are who you say you are."

The platforms supported by this feature are Twitter, Facebook, and Google, and this section covers all three.

Regardless of which platform is used, Zendesk will never have access to the customer's password for that service.

The social logins are enabled on the End Users tab of the "Security administration" page. Enabling each of the options is a simple process of selecting the relevant checkbox and saving the tab. When you enable each of the social media platforms, customers will immediately see that platform listed on the sign-in page, as an alternative to entering a Zendesk username and password. Figure 3-1 demonstrates an example with the logins for Twitter, Facebook, and Google enabled.

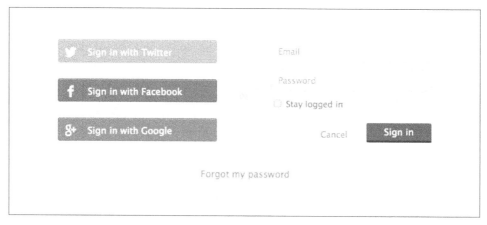

Figure 3-1. Sign-in page displayed to users when the social media logins are enabled

In order for users to sign in using one of these tools, they must be able to authenticate with that service. This process relies on standardized security mechanisms (in the case of Twitter, this is OAuth) to ensure the security and safety of your user accounts. The Twitter sign-in page is shown in Figure 3-2, which clearly indicates the permissions that the user is authorizing for Zendesk to use, and reiterates that Zendesk does not have access to the user's Twitter password. When the user authenticates in this way, Zendesk also does not have access to post to the user's Twitter timeline, so there'll be no "Erin has just signed into Zendesk" posted to the Twittersphere. These same concepts also apply to the Facebook and Google sign-in options.

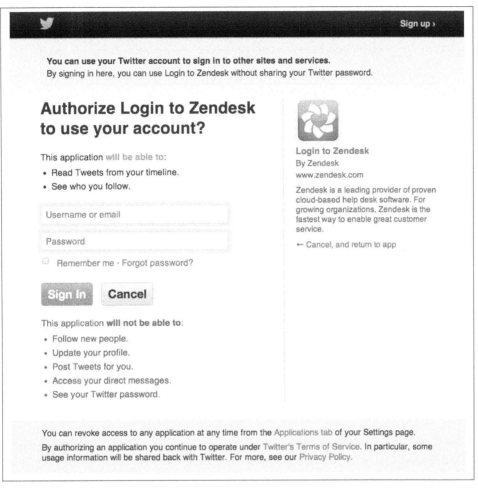

Figure 3-2. Twitter's authentication screen with the list of permissions requested

When a user successfully authenticates with the social media service, he will be signed in to Zendesk, and Zendesk will create a user account for him automatically. If the user has signed in using Twitter or Facebook, Zendesk will immediately prompt him to enter an email address. Zendesk relies on email heavily for its communication with users, which is the reason why an email address is required at this stage. In fact, users cannot proceed with using Zendesk—even after signing in—until they have provided an email address. In the case of the Google social media login, Zendesk will be notified of the user's email address by Google automatically, so the user will not be prompted separately for his email address.

From an administrator's perspective, it's impossible to tell whether a user is choosing to authenticate using a social media service, or if he has a password configured in Zendesk.

When you look at a user's profile, you'll see if his Twitter, Facebook, or Google account is linked to his Zendesk user profile, but as far as you're concerned, he could be using any one of the available mechanisms to sign in.

In general, this feature is useful, and worth leveraging as a convenience to your users. We don't believe the level of risk introduced by integrating with these external platforms is high enough to warrant steering clear of the service.

Suspended Tickets

Zendesk has a number of rules to determine which tickets should be suspended. Examples of these rules include spam, emails from unauthorized users, emails from unverified users, out-of-office replies, mail loops, and automated notifications. Zendesk does not delete these tickets completely (unless the spam filter identifies an email as 99.9% likely to be spam), but places them in a view called *suspended tickets* (views are covered in more depth on page 119). It is the responsibility of your support agents to periodically review this list of suspended tickets and take appropriate action. There is currently no way to disable the conditions for suspending tickets, either globally or individually.

If you or another member of your team would like to be alerted by email when tickets are added to the suspended tickets list, there is an option named Suspended Ticket Notifications in the Tickets administration page, which offers an email digest every 10 minutes, every hour, or once per day. The recipients of the alert can be any email address, and are not restricted to users who already exist in your Zendesk instance.

The Suspended Ticket Notification feature adds peace of mind that unimportant emails will be filtered out of your ticket inbox, but it's still a good idea to have your agents check the suspended tickets list periodically. You can think of the list as similar to your junk email inbox. Like your junk email inbox, most of the contents of the suspended tickets list will have a valid reason for being suspended, so checking the list once per day is usually frequent enough. The occasional ticket that gets caught erroneously can wait until tomorrow to receive a response from your support team.

For your agents, working with items in the suspended tickets list is quite simple, and every agent in Zendesk will have access to the suspended tickets view. On a regular basis, ask your agents to open the suspended tickets view (it is the only view that appears in red), and browse the contents. If they find an item that looks like it shouldn't be suspended, your agents can recover it *automatically* or *manually*. Automatic recovery is a one-step process but does not allow any changes to the ticket, and manual recovery allows the agent to update the ticket before submitting it. An example of a suspended ticket is shown in Figure 3-3. This item shows an automated response from an email server, which states that the target address for an email notification from Zendesk was invalid. Because this message from the email server is classified as an automated reply and this is one of the reasons for suspension, the email was added to the suspended tickets list.

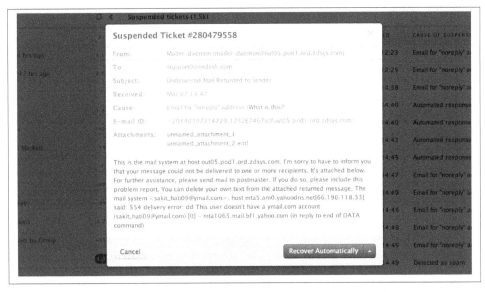

Figure 3-3. Example of a suspended ticket, including all information fields

Depending on the exact reason for suspension, Zendesk offers a variety of actions that an agent can take to recover the suspended ticket. In some cases, the issue is related to user accounts, so Zendesk will offer to create the user account while recovering the ticket. Zendesk may offer to add the email as a comment on an existing ticket or create a new ticket. Most of these options are intuitive. It's also easy to perform the operations in bulk by selecting multiple checkboxes on the main suspended tickets list, including deletion of all tickets marked as suspended.

Public Creation of User Profiles

Probably one of the biggest decisions you'll make about user management in Zendesk is whether to let your clients create their own user profiles. If you are working for a company with a broad or anonymous user base and you don't know the names and email addresses of all those users, it makes sense for you to enable *open* access to your Zendesk instance. In this situation, if users are seeking support, they can simply visit your Help Center and create a new profile to submit a ticket.

The other option for user profile creation is to use the *closed* option, and there are two situations in which you might decide to use this:

Restricting ticket submission to known users

If you're confident that you have a comprehensive list of user accounts, it's possible for administrators to create those user accounts in the system (which can be automated using a CSV import), thereby restricting ticket submission to only those users. This would be useful if you want to ensure that support is provided to known users only. It ensures less work on behalf of agents, who won't need to filter through invalid support requests, but slightly more work on behalf of administrators, who will need to create all of those user accounts before your customers can sign in.

Dove-tailing with SSO

If you elect to use single sign-on (see "Integrating with an External User Database" on page 30), you might also elect to disable public creation of user profiles. This may not necessarily prevent any member of the public from submitting tickets (because that will depend on the way your SSO is configured), but it delegates the selection of who can submit those tickets to users who have an account in your company's user database. If you have an existing list of members on your web application, for example, you can set up Zendesk to ensure that only the users in the web application database can create support tickets. Anyone else who wants to submit a ticket must create a profile with your web application to get access to your Zendesk instance.

A closed Zendesk instance does not allow the Feedback Tab channel (covered on page 63) to work, and all incoming emails from addresses not already in the system will be immediately added to the suspended tickets list (covered on page 28).

Integrating with an External User Database

Single sign-on (SSO) is a system that allows you to connect the Zendesk user database with an external user management system. Some companies like to save their users the effort of maintaining several sets of sign-in information (a problem that leads people to keep long lists of user account names and passwords written on insecure pieces of paper at their desks), so they elect to use SSO. Implementation of this option requires some programming and is outside the scope of this book, though you can find more information in the Zendesk knowledge base article on the topic (*http://bit.ly/sso-opt*).

To enable or disable public access to your Zendesk instance, open the Customers administration page. The relevant option on this page is "Anybody can submit tickets," and it is selected by default. If you leave this option selected, you'll have an open Zendesk instance where anyone in the world can sign up with an end-user profile and submit tickets. A sample of the form displayed to the user (with CAPTCHA enabled) is shown in Figure 3-4. If you uncheck the "Anybody can submit tickets" option, you'll have a closed Zendesk instance.

Sign up to Blue Skies

Please fill out this form, and we'll send you a welcome email to
verify your email address and log you in.

Your full name *

Your email *

Please verify text *

42 **89643665**

Two other words please   I want audio instead

Cancel   **Sign up**

Figure 3-4. Sign-up page on an open Zendesk instance

After you've enabled the open Zendesk instance option, you'll be presented with another set of options. The option labeled "Ask users to register" simply means that anyone can submit a ticket, but that the ticket will be marked as suspended until that user verifies her account and email address. This is a kind of middle ground between the open and closed user profile option, which ensures that everyone can submit a ticket, but only users who are willing to verify that they've entered a valid email address will have their tickets viewed by a support agent.

 To most Zendesk administrators, it should be obvious whether they have intimate knowledge of their customer base or not, leading to the decision about whether your Zendesk instance should allow public creation of user profiles. Our recommendation is this: if you don't have a complete customer list or if you're not sure who will be contacting you, start by allowing public creation of user profiles, use some of the methods described later in this book to automatically triage certain requests, and then disable public profile creation at a later date if you find that you're just getting too many invalid requests.

Blacklists and Whitelists

If you've enabled public access to your Zendesk instance, you still have several more levels of control over the people who can submit tickets in Zendesk. The blacklist and whitelist are used to define rules that determine which emails should be accepted or rejected when they are received in your Zendesk instance. To find the blacklist and whitelist settings, open the Customers administration page and make sure that the "Anybody can submit tickets" option is enabled.

There are several common scenarios for using the blacklist and whitelist:

Limited customer list

If you would like to accept incoming emails from only a limited set of customers, you can use the blacklist to block *all* emails, then the whitelist to create a limited number of exceptions. To achieve this, enter an asterisk (*) in the blacklist, and a comma-separated list of email addresses or email domains in the whitelist.

Problem customers

If you find that a certain email address or domain name is sending emails that you do not want to receive in your Zendesk instance, you can include these in the blacklist without entering any values in the whitelist. The message here is simply "reject anything in the blacklist, but accept everything else." If you would like to specify a domain name, the format should be just the domain and the suffix (e.g., *company.com*, not **.company.com* or another variation).

Valid notifications

Since automated email notices are suspended based on the standard rules of suspension, notifications that are sent from Google or other online services will typically be suspended. If these notifications are important for your company and should be accepted and processed normally, simply enter the email addresses or domains of the valid email senders in the whitelist field, and these addresses will no longer be suspended with the other automated emails. In this scenario it is possible to enter values in the whitelist without using the blacklist, although you can still use the blacklist for limiting the customer list or dealing with problem customers.

Disabling email entirely

If you have decided that no users should be able to email your support team and that any emails received should be rejected immediately without suspension, it's possible for you to enter the keyword `reject:*` in the blacklist, which will achieve this. If you were to just enter an asterisk (*) in the blacklist without the `reject:` prefix, all emails would be suspended. The `reject` keyword bypasses the suspended tickets list altogether.

The blacklist and whitelist deal with emails only, and do not prohibit users with these email addresses from creating a user profile in Zendesk and submitting a ticket manually.

Password Strength Policy

There are three options for managing the strength of user passwords in Zendesk, and you can set a password security level for end users separate from the password policy for your agents and administrators. In other words, you might be less concerned with the security of your end-user passwords than the passwords used by your agents and administrators. After all, your support team has access to your Zendesk data and system settings. Here are the options you can use:

Low
> This option requires your users to select a password with at least five characters, and no other restrictions are applied. Some people criticize this option for being too weak, but many people like this option because they believe that most users are capable of managing their own rules for password complexity.

Medium
> This option requires all passwords to be at least six characters, which must include mixed-case letters, numbers, and a character that is not a letter or number. It's a good middle-ground option, which enforces simple requirements on the users. Let's face it: any password these days that does not include characters other than letters is probably not a very secure password anyway.

High
> The final option requires users to change their password every 90 days, a condition that is often criticized. Many IT folks say that this is considered *less* secure, because users tend to write their new passwords somewhere, which introduces the risk of someone else finding the password. Aside from this rule, the other conditions are that the password cannot be one of the previous five passwords used, and that it must have the same complexity rules as the Medium level. It's up to you to decide whether you think that this is truly the most secure option for your Zendesk instance, and if the requirement for users to change their password every 90 days is a worthwhile inconvenience.

Whichever options you choose for your support team and your end users, the separate password settings are available on the Admins & Agents and End Users tabs on the Security administration page. After you select one of the options from the list of radio buttons, click the Save tab and the new policy will be applied immediately. If you decrease the policy, existing users will be unaffected. If you increase the policy, all users will have up to five days to change their password, after which time they will be forced to change their password the next time they sign into your Zendesk instance.

Secure Sockets Layer (SSL)

To ensure the privacy and security of your customers, we strongly encourage you to enable SSL on your Zendesk instance. The reason is that SSL ensures that all data transmitted through your browser is encrypted, and any attempts by intruders to intercept the data transfer are less likely to be successful.

Fortunately, SSL is enabled by default on all Zendesk instances. If, for whatever reason, you would like to disable SSL, you can change the setting in the Global tab on the Security administration page. This page also has a notice that discourages you from disabling SSL.

If you followed the instructions earlier in this book to set up a custom URL (e.g., *support.blueskies.com*), you may notice that the Zendesk URL reverts to your default URL (e.g., *<companyname>.zendesk.com*) when the browser switches to the HTTPS protocol (HTTPS is the protocol used when SSL is active). The reason is that in order for SSL to work, your browser requires a certificate that matches the domain name of the URL being opened. Zendesk has a certificate for its own domain name, so any visits to a subdomain of *zendesk.com* will use the Zendesk certificate. If you change your domain name to *support.blueskies.com*, the browser can no longer use the *zendesk.com* certificate to validate the URL, and must use a certificate for *blueskies.com* instead. To guarantee the security of your Zendesk instance when SSL is enabled on a custom URL, Zendesk will always switch back to the *<companyname>.zendesk.com* URL unless you take some further steps.

To ensure that your custom URL shows in every situation, you'll first need to be on the Plus or Enterprise plans. If you are, you'll need to generate an SSL certificate for your custom URL with a third-party provider. Most webmasters should have the knowledge required to perform this task. The first step is to visit the Global tab on the Security administration page inside Zendesk. If you have a custom URL enabled, there will be a link on this page to generate a Certificate Signing Request (CSR). The CSR is a file that your webmaster will use to generate the certificate for your custom domain name, and you should download it from this page and provide it to the person who can generate an SSL certificate with the third party. After the certificate has been generated, you should visit the Global tab on the Security administration page in Zendesk again to upload your SSL certificate. The certificate will be installed manually by the Zendesk operations team, which can take a few days, and once the process is complete you'll receive an email with details on next steps.

While you're waiting for the certificate to be installed, there's no problem with running your Zendesk instance on a *<company-name>.zendesk.com* URL. Users will still be able to start by visiting your custom URL, but Zendesk will redirect them to the more secure URL as it deems necessary to guarantee a secure connection.

Enterprise Security and Compliance

On the Plus and Enterprise plans, customers are able to control Zendesk user access based on the IP address of the visitor. A typical use case for this feature is when you need to restrict access to people who are physically located in your office. Alternatively, a user can connect to a virtual private network (VPN) to access your corporate network securely first, and then open Zendesk from that IP address, and it will appear as if she is connecting from your office network. The options to control user access can be found in the Global tab on the Security administration page.

Access can be restricted globally for all user accounts, but this is often useful only if you're running an internal customer service solution and your end users are also members of your team. This is the default setting when access restriction is enabled.

Access can also be set to restrict just agent and administrator accounts, which is useful in a broader range of Zendesk environments because it still allows customers all over the world to submit tickets. Put simply, this means that if an administrator wants to change a Zendesk configuration setting, or an agent wants to read the complete list of tickets, he must be physically located in your office. To enable this option, click the checkbox for "Customers can bypass restrictions."

When you enable this feature, the restriction will also have an impact on API calls by external applications, including the mobile apps. If your agents need to use the Zendesk mobile apps from any location, the final option on the Global tab is "Agents can access via mobile apps," which will allow them to do this.

Email Archiving

The other compliance feature required by some heavily regulated organizations or industries is the ability to blind carbon copy (BCC) absolutely every email notification from Zendesk to a specific email address. This option is named Email Archiving on the Tickets administration page, and is available only for customers on the Enterprise plan. The use case for this feature is when a company, for regulatory or compliance reasons, needs an archived copy of all email communication with users. For most other companies, this is an unnecessary feature.

Audit Log

Also available to administrators on the Enterprise plan is a feature called the Audit Log. It monitors changes to important settings and other actions in your Zendesk instance, such as the creation of new agents and administrators, changes made to an agent's role, password policy changes, deleted tickets, and so on. It tracks who made a change and when it was made, which provides you with an easy way to monitor changes that may affect the security of your Zendesk instance.

You'll find this feature on the Account administration page by clicking the Audit Log tab. There's no configuration required for the audit log; it's enabled by default and cannot be turned off (not something you'd want to do anyway). Some of the changes (e.g., a new administrator being added to your Zendesk instance) will also cause an email notification to be sent to every administrator. It is possible to configure who receives the email notifications: it can be all administrators (the default), the account owner, or a specific agent group. If you're on the Enterprise plan, the Audit Log feature is one you'll want to routinely monitor to ensure that, from a security perspective, everything is in order.

Agent Device Management

Another security feature, available on all Zendesk plans, is Device Management. This is similar to the Audit Log in the sense that it is always on and tracks events in your Zendesk instance that may affect security. It's different, however, in that not all administrators are notified of events. Instead, device management tracks the devices that have been used to sign in to your Zendesk instance using your sign-in credentials (your Zendesk account email address and password) and displays this information just to you in your user profile.

A tab in your user profile called Devices & Apps lists all the computers (including smartphones and tablets) and browsers used to sign in to your account. You'll see the device used, the geographic location where the access occurred, and the date it occurred. You'll also see any third-party applications that were used to access your Zendesk instance using your sign-in credentials. Receiving email notifications when a device is added is optional, and you'll see a toggle to turn notifications on or off.

If you ever have any concerns that someone else has used your sign-in credentials to access your account, this is the place to check, and we recommend that you do so occasionally as part of your secure computing best practices.

CHAPTER 4

User Management

Anyone who interacts with your Zendesk instance, in one way or another, will have a user profile. The extent to which your customers use their user profile will differ greatly. Some customers like to sign into the Zendesk Help Center and customize their profile when they're getting support from your company. Others prefer to sign in but don't care to update their name or upload a photo. Other customers may never sign into your Help Center, preferring instead to interact using one of the external channels, such as email, Twitter, Facebook, or Voice.

Regardless of the level of interaction, every person who interacts will have a user profile, and that user profile will be classified as an end user, an agent, or an administrator. Each of these levels is described in this chapter.

All user management is done from the People administration page in Zendesk, with just a few links at the top of the page (shown in Figure 4-1). The section at the top of the page can also be used to search for users and to filter the results shown on the People administration page.

Figure 4-1. User management functions on the People administration page

Administrators

Every new Zendesk instance is created with one administrator user account. The details of that account (name and email address) must be entered by the person who originally set up the Zendesk instance. The first administrator is also called the *account owner* of the Zendesk instance, and she is the only user who can make changes to the billing details and plan of the instance. If you'd like to change the account owner of your Zendesk instance, you can do so by going to the Invoices tab on the "Account administration" page and selecting another administrator in your Zendesk instance.

To add an administrator in the product, select the "user" link from the People administration page, and then select Administrator as the user type. If you're on the Enterprise plan, the process will differ slightly (refer to "Adding an Agent on the Enterprise Plan" on page 48).

Limiting the Number of Administrators

Technically, there's no limit on the number of administrator accounts that you can create in Zendesk, but we advise against using any more than three administrator accounts. We often see IT companies with a team full of people with the technical competence to administer a Zendesk instance. However, although they may be *technically* competent, it's difficult for more than three people to communicate effectively with one another on proposed administrative and business process changes—and communication is an important aspect of managing a cohesive administrative design for Zendesk.

Small Zendesk instances might have one or two administrators, and large instances should stick to the three administrator limit. Even if you have a thousand agents, it's still very difficult for four or five or six administrators to stay synchronized on the administrative design.

Having a smaller number of administrators is also a recommended practice to improve security. *Phishing* is a social engineering technique used by hackers to gain unauthorized access to your username and password. The smaller the number of users with access to administer your Zendesk instance, the better your chances of preventing one of these attacks.

Agents and Roles

Agents are the people on your team who provide support to your customers. Every agent is a paid account in the system, and every agent will have greater permissions in your Zendesk instance than your customers. Agents are trusted with the privacy and security of your customers, but most importantly, they are trusted with your company's customer service reputation.

Groups

Groups are a simple way to collect agent accounts together, for a wide range of purposes that will become obvious as examples are given throughout this book. Agents can belong to several groups, and the choice of groups is made when you add an agent. It's also possible for an administrator to add or remove agents from groups at any time.

Adding a group is very simple. In fact, there are almost no configurable options for adding a group. The reason is that group configurations are spread throughout the product, not the other way around. As an example, visibility of views (covered in more depth on page 119) can be limited to only a specific group. Another example is a trigger (you can find more information about triggers on page 132) that would assign new tickets to a specific group according to relevant criteria. But the most common example is that groups will appear in the Assignee field on the ticket screen as a funnel into a subset of agents to which the ticket should be assigned.

Zendesk doesn't support hierarchies of groups, but it's possible for every agent to belong to more than one group. For example, if you create a group for Level 1 Support and another group for Level 2 Support, you cannot categorize the latter as a subgroup of the former, but it is possible to add an agent to both groups.

To create a new group, open the People administration page, then click the "group" link beside the word "add" in the upper-right corner of the page. The user creation form will ask for the name of the group and allow you to select which agents should be added into the group. Select "Create group" when you're finished. This will immediately create the group, which is ready to be used in some of the ways just listed.

Defining Groups

Each organization defines its groups differently. Generally speaking, your groups can be informally classified by their use as follows:

Funneling
> On the ticket screen, the Assignee field will include both groups and agents. If one of your agents would like to escalate a ticket to a member of your user interface development team but doesn't know the specific members of that team, she can select the User Interface Development group in the Assignee field. After this group is selected, the Assignee field will drill down to include just the members of that group. The agent then has the option to select the entire group by clicking User Interface Development again, or selecting one of the specific agents in the group. To accommodate this use of groups, as an administrator you should create a group for every team that can feasibly handle tickets in your organization.

Sharing

As described in "Views" on page 119 and "Macros" on page 124 later, it's possible to create views and macros, then share them with specific agents, meaning that those agents can access the views and macros directly. The agents with whom the rules are shared will all need to belong to the same group. So if you want to share a view with your entire product team, you should create a group called Development Team so that you can easily share it. Combining this with funneling, you now have a set of at least two groups: User Interface Development and Development Team.

Permissions

If you'd like to restrict access of certain Zendesk features to various team members, you can use groups to achieve this. One example is the Twitter channel (covered on page 69), which allows you to restrict the Twitter feature to authorized users only. Because Twitter is typically a feature that would be used by your marketing team, you might create a Marketing group, the members of which are the only users who can use the Twitter feature.

Business process

"Triggers" on page 132 and "Automations" on page 140 provide several examples of business rules that leverage groups to assign, reassign, or escalate tickets. The groups that you define for this purpose might be specific to the use case. For example, if you're defining an escalation process using automation, you might set up a Development Team Managers group.

It's very likely that a single group will meet several of these criteria. For example, a Development Team Managers group could simultaneously be used to manually escalate a ticket via the ticket screen (funneling), support sharing of views to find all tickets that have been escalated (sharing), and work in conjunction with a business rule (business process).

Agent Signatures

Similar to most email applications, Zendesk allows all agents to include a unique signature at the end of every comment they add to tickets. From an administrator's perspective, it is often important to build a level of consistency into the format of these signatures, which is a setting that is configured on the Agents administration page.

You can format an agent's signature using Markdown, a simple text formatting syntax that allows you to create headings and bullet lists, apply bold and italic formatting, and so on. Markdown can also be used to insert your company logo into the signature. Markdown is applied to plain text and then displayed to your customers as HTML.

The agent signature will be visible in the Help Center as well as outgoing email correspondence, but it will not be appended to comments added to tickets created via the Twitter or Facebook channels.

To configure the standard template for your agents' signatures, you will need to edit the Signature option on the Agents administration page. By default, this field contains the text {{agent.signature}}. This is another example of a *placeholder* (described in more detail in "Placeholders" on page 150); the code shown here will be replaced by the individual agent's signature.

It is the administrator's responsibility to add the extra pieces of text that are not included in the individual agent's signature. A very common example would be the company slogan, or some useful information about hours of support (e.g., "Phone support offered 9 a.m. to 5 p.m., Monday through Friday; email support at other times"). Again, this information will appear at the bottom of every comment added to a ticket, and it's very likely that your customers will read this information.

We've seen advertisements used in this space, but you should be careful not to make customers feel like you don't take their support requests seriously. Customers can be very frustrated during the support process, and telling them about the new 3D version of your widget might just frustrate them more.

Adding an Agent Account

The steps that you'll follow to create an agent account on the Starter, Regular, and Plus plans will differ slightly from the steps on the Enterprise plan. The topics in this section cover the first method.

First, the pricing model of Zendesk requires you to pay a fee for every agent account in your instance. End-user accounts are free. So basically, you should create an agent account only for people who need to sign in to the system to answer support requests, publish content to your knowledge base, or run reports as a manager. Also, administrator accounts are counted as agent accounts for the purposes of billing.

To create an agent account, open the People administration page, then click the "user" link beside "add" in the upper-right corner of the page. You are then prompted to enter the user's name and email address as well as choose his role as agent. After you've done that and clicked the Save button, the new user's profile page will appear. Most of the options on this page—such as Phone, Time zone, Language, Details, and Notes—are self-explanatory. If you're using the Plus or Enterprise plans, there will be a field labeled Alias, which is the name that will be displayed to end users instead of the agent's real name. This feature is provided mostly for privacy of the agent, and some customers use this field to abbreviate the agent's last name. For example, Stafford Vaughan might have an alias in Zendesk of "Stafford V."

The "role" listed on the user creation page is different from the "role" functionality available on the Enterprise plan, which is explained in "Enterprise Agent Roles and Light Agents" on page 42.

When "agent" is selected as the user's role, the user's profile will contain profile options that are not added to an end user's profile. The options include a list of groups of which the agent will be a member, the agent's access to tickets within your Zendesk instance, the option for the agent to publish comments that are visible to your customers, and whether she has Help Center viewer or manager privileges. Help Center managers are users who can edit or delete any article in your Help Center. Even if you don't grant this permission to your agent, you can allow agents to edit the articles in sections of your knowledge base that you have explicitly given them permission for. This is discussed in more detail later in the book.

The option to restrict agent access to tickets will be discussed in "Restricting Agent Access to Tickets" on page 117, but our general recommendation is that agents have access to all tickets.

By default, your new agents are placed into the Support group (this is a group that is added to every Zendesk instance). This is because a group is required to assign and solve a ticket. As you add groups to your Zendesk instance, you can add your agents to other groups and set one of those other groups as the default group so that the next time you add an agent he will be assigned to that default group.

Enterprise Agent Roles and Light Agents

One of the best features of the Enterprise plan is the ability to configure agent permissions at a more granular level than the Starter, Regular, or Plus plans. This feature is known as *agent roles* (or sometimes just *roles*). The process of adding a new agent to your Zendesk instance on the Starter, Regular, and Plus plans provides the administrator with four different options (listed in the previous section), but the Agent Roles feature on the Enterprise plan extends this list to 20 different options, each of which is described in "Configuration Options for Agent Roles" on page 44. To make the management of these options more convenient, Zendesk captures the selected options in a single role, which can then be assigned to a specific set of agents.

Out of the box, Zendesk comes with five roles already defined. To find these roles, click the "roles" link beneath the search box on the People administration page. A quick summary of each of these roles is as follows:

Administrator

This is a special role that replaces the administrator user type on the other plans. On the Enterprise plan, the options for the Administrator role cannot be customized.

Light Agent

Like Administrator, this is a special role with limited options for customization. The purpose of this role is to allow team members outside the support team at your organization to sign in and *assist* the support process. Light Agents can never update the fields in a ticket, which means that they cannot solve a ticket, assign a ticket, add tags, or anything else. The only task that can be performed by a Light Agent is to add a private comment to a ticket, which is a comment that will be visible only to other members of your support organization. A common situation in which you'd use this feature would be when you involve your development team in the process of solving a customer's support inquiry, especially if it was related to a bug in your software. Another example is a finance team, who would provide status updates on financial matters. In both of these cases, private comments will be added to a ticket by the development and finance teams, and it is the responsibility of the support agent to pass on the relevant information to the customer, and maintain the status of the ticket.

Staff

This is the standard role that you would assign to your support team. The default configuration of this role is quite restrictive, so we usually recommend changing some of the default settings for this role. In particular, you should probably change this role from restricting access to tickets in the agent's groups to allowing access to all tickets instead.

Team Leader

This is not a special role, and seems to be mostly added for example purposes. This role is useful for someone who should have slightly higher access than most support team members, which would usually be, as the name suggests, a team leader.

Advisor

This is also a role that is mostly for example purposes, but might typically be used for an agent who should have some administrative privileges, but not all. This is typically someone who will not be solving support requests but who assists administrators with defining business rules or provides guidance on other Zendesk settings. Unless you have a large team of administrators or a very large customer service team, you probably don't need to use the Advisors role and can delete it.

Legacy Agent

This is a special role for organizations that upgrade from the Starter, Regular, or Plus plans to the Enterprise plan. When you upgrade, Zendesk does not automatically assume that all of your agents should be granted one of the Enterprise roles listed in this section. Instead, all existing agents are assigned to the *Legacy Agent* role, and will have the same permissions as the previous plan. I recommend that after you upgrade, you immediately open your agent profiles and move your agents onto one of the dedicated roles in Enterprise, if for no reason other than to take advantage of the granularity of those roles. After you move your agents into one of the newer roles, it's impossible to move them back onto the Legacy Agent role.

Agents using the Light Agent role are completely free, which I consider to be the very best feature of the Enterprise plan. Because these accounts are free, Enterprise customers often add every member of their organization as a Light Agent inside Zendesk, which means that all conversations about support tickets will stay inside Zendesk, rather than conversations with the development or finance team being scattered in email.

Configuration Options for Agent Roles

For each role, there are approximately 20 individual options to be configured. Most of the options are self-explanatory, but the decision process for each option is not always so obvious. In the following list, we explain some of the more common considerations for these options, in the context of the other features explained in this book.

What kind of tickets can this agent access?

This option is discussed in "Restricting Agent Access to Tickets" on page 117.

Agent can assign to any group

If you specifically select the "All within the agent's group(s)" option in the "What kind of tickets can this agent access?" drop-down list, a new option will pop up that allows you to determine whether the agent can assign a ticket to groups other than those of which she is a member. By default, this is unchecked. The problem with leaving it unchecked is that the agent cannot escalate a ticket to whichever group is necessary. On the other hand, leaving it unchecked prevents agents from lobbing tickets away from their group, if they don't want to take care of it themselves. I would err on the side of the first choice, which is to enable this option to give more control to agents, and trust them to make a wise decision as to whether the ticket is suited for their group. (Perhaps those are famous last words.)

What type of comments can this agent make?

To put it simply, some people just shouldn't be making publicly visible comments on tickets. You've probably met someone like this—the person who is less than diplomatic with difficult customers. Most customer service team members have the necessary skills to be polite or, at the very least, professional. If you've opened up your Zendesk instance to other teams (e.g., the development, finance, or marketing teams), those customer service skills may not necessarily exist. I don't want to stereotype, but I do encourage you to limit direct customer access to the pros, and enable public comments just for your trained customer service team.

Can edit ticket properties

This option can be used to restrict agents to read-only access on tickets. The functionality is very similar to the Light Agent role, but if you create a custom role for this purpose instead of using Light Agents, the benefit is that you can provide other privileges to the user. If this option is disabled, the next three options in this list will not be enabled. If you've disabled this option, you should also consider allowing these agents to add only private comments (see the previous item in this list), which means that the agent is restricted to communicating internally within your organization only.

Can delete tickets

This option does exactly what it suggests. You should be aware that there is no audit trail of deleted tickets in Zendesk, so this privilege should be given sparingly.

Can merge tickets

There aren't many compelling reasons to prevent agents from merging tickets, because merging a ticket is a relatively innocuous task. As a side effect of merging tickets, one ticket will be closed for further comments, but it's still possible to create a follow-up for that ticket.

Can edit ticket tags

Some organizations elect to link specific tags very closely to strict business processes, and therefore the tags should not be editable by agents. For example, a tag of "vip" might be so important to your organization that it would be damaging to allow an agent to add this tag to arbitrary tickets. If this is the case, you should disable the tagging privilege using this checkbox. Otherwise, agent tagging is a very useful feature that supports a great many functions in the product, and we encourage you to enable this feature for your agents.

What access does this agent have to end-user profiles?

If there is a very strict list of end users to whom you should provide support, you might want to use this option to prevent agents from creating new end-user accounts arbitrarily. On the Starter, Regular, and Plus plans, agents are trusted to be able to create end-user accounts. If you're on the Enterprise plan and have access to the roles function, you could use this option to prevent agents from adding new user profiles.

May this user view lists of user profiles?

It's not possible to block agents from viewing the details of individual end-user profiles, regardless of the plan you're using. Using this option, it *is* possible to prevent agents from finding user profiles en masse, or prevent them from searching for user profiles. If you disable this option, agents may use the user's profile link on a ticket only as a channel to find out further information about the user.

What can this agent do with customer lists?

Customer lists are collections of customers that you define based on system attributes, tags, and custom fields. They are similar to what views are for tickets. As with the previous permission, if you want to prevent your agents from viewing customer data and user profiles, you disable this option.

Can add or modify groups & organizations

If the option "What access does this agent have to end-user profiles?" is configured to give agents the privilege to create new user profiles in Zendesk, the option to also modify groups and organizations will appear to the administrator. The organization portion of this option is particularly useful, because it allows agents to create organizations to categorize end users. It also allows the agent to add groups and include fellow agents into those groups, so there's a high amount of trust involved in granting this privilege to agents.

Can manage Help Center

Administrators, and agents given this permission, are responsible for managing the Help Center, which means setting up the structure of the knowledge and community, defining user acccess, and customizing the design.

What can this agent do with reports?

Zendesk has a reporting feature that shows simple reports to agents and administrators. It's a good idea to share this information with agents, because it allows them to make informed decisions, particularly if there is a spike in a certain area. A high-level view of the status of your customer service team might be more information than you're willing to share, though, and if it is, you can use this option to prevent agents from viewing reports.

What can this agent do with views/macros?

We've grouped the separate options for views and macros into the same item here, because the same principles apply to both. They share first place for our favorite option for roles. Basically, they allow administrators to delegate the responsibility of creating agent rules to the agents themselves. Later in this book, in "Shared Views" on page 123 and "Adding a Shared Macro" on page 125, we explain how to share these features with your agents if you're an administrator, but if you're on the Enterprise plan, these rules are instantly democratized for your agents.

Can access dynamic content

If you have a small list of agents whom you trust to publish reusable content for all users, this option allows you to grant that privilege to those agents. Dynamic content was explained in "Dynamic Content for Text Translation" on page 17, but we mentioned that it's typically the domain of the administrators to create new strings of text. If you enable this option, you're effectively allowing your agents to assist with the translation process.

Can answer chat requests

For the same reasons described earlier in the discussion of restricting agent access to public comments, it might be worth preventing some of your agents from taking chat requests. This just ensures that the right people for the job are interacting with your customers directly.

Can access Twitter saved searches

Because Twitter is a very public communication medium, it's generally a good idea to restrict Twitter access to users who have demonstrated an understanding of its sensitive nature. As described in "Twitter" on page 69, an accidentally published tweet can have very negative consequences for your brand's reputation.

Can manage Facebook Pages

If you've set up a group of agents who will be managing your social media presence but you'd prefer not to give those users full administrative privileges to your Zendesk instance, use this option.

Can answer phone calls

Similar to the concept of chat and public comments, this feature allows you to restrict phone privileges to only certain agents. Some people are just better on the phone than other people.

Can manage business rules

If you trust some of your agents to manage your customer service workflow but would rather not give them full administrative access to your Zendesk instance, enabling this option for those agents is a good compromise. By using this option to give workflow access to particular agents, you and the other administrators can focus on more important features of your Zendesk instance (e.g., security).

Can manage channels and extensions

If you have some team members who are technically inclined and who manage the integrations on your Zendesk instance, then you might decide to give them this privilege, without giving them full administrative access. Just like the "can manage business rules" option, this is a compromise, and supports the idea of spreading the administrative load without foregoing control over the security of your system.

Adding an Agent on the Enterprise Plan

Now that you've configured your roles and selected the options for each role, the process to add an agent on the Enterprise plan is quite similar to adding an agent on the other plans. The first step is to click the "user" link next to the "add" section on the People administration page. The only difference between this process on the Enterprise plan and the other plans is that when you're prompted to enter the agent's name and email address and to select his role, you'll see the end user, administrator, and all the Enterprise agent roles listed in the drop-down (not just the standard end user, agent, and administrator roles).

End-User Access

End users are usually your customers (although in the case of an internal customer support environment, they may be colleagues), and they will be the people who are seeking help. It's possible in Zendesk to grant end users access to more than just their own tickets, though you must take into account some important considerations around privacy before enabling this setting.

The most common method by which end users are created in Zendesk is that a person creates his own account via the "sign up" link in your Help Center. Alternatively, end-user accounts may be automatically created when a new email is received in your Zendesk instance. For the situations in which the person has not created his own account, this section will explain how to create an end-user account as an administrator.

Creating an End User

Just like creating an agent and administrator, creating an end user involves clicking the "user" link next to the "add" section on the People administration page. There is a slight difference with adding end users, which is that some agents—depending on their permissions—can perform this function as well as administrators. The end-user fields are a subset of the fields that are included in an agent's profile. For example, the Alias field will not appear for end users. End users are also much more likely to have a value in the Organization field, which is explained in "Organizations" on page 52.

 A shortcut method of creating end-user accounts is available to agents during the process of adding a ticket, which is very convenient when the ticket requester does not already exist in the system. This process presents only a few core fields to the agent, just for the sake of simplicity. If an end user is created using this method, it's always a good practice to visit the end user's profile again at a later date and ensure that all fields for this user account have been set correctly.

Bulk-Importing Users

Another method for adding agents and end users to your Zendesk instance is a bulk import of user profiles. You may have done this in other SaaS business applications you've used and therefore may already be familiar with how this works.

Start by creating a CSV file containing your list of users. Most people start their list in a spreadsheet program such as Microsoft Excel or OpenOffice.org Calc and then save it as a CSV file, which formats the rows and columns of the spreadsheet as plain text with column values separated by a comma and each row (or record) terminated by a newline in the file. Upload the CSV file into Zendesk, which will match the columns to fields in the user profile and create new user accounts with all the parameters you specify. Of course, you need to create a spreadsheet that matches the exact order required by Zendesk to successfully map the data into the correct user profile fields.

You can also use this method to import a list of organizations into your Zendesk instance. In fact, you'll need to do that first if you use organizations because they need to be there before you bulk-import your list of users. The details of the bulk-import process are described in the Zendesk knowledge base article on the subject (*http://bit.ly/bulk-import*).

Merging End Users

When you're using multiple channels to provide support to your customers, you'll occasionally have a situation where the same person submits a ticket for a single topic using several different channels. As an example, your customer might start by tweeting her concern, then escalate her inquiry by sending an email, then call into your Voice phone number if she does not receive a timely response with the other channels. Because each channel is different, every new submission from the same customer will be a separate ticket with a separate ticket ID, and—if the user profile does not already exist in Zendesk—the requester of each of these tickets will also be a different user profile in the system. This becomes difficult to manage from an agent's perspective because he must search through several user accounts to find tickets from the same person, and it's a problem for customers because they could potentially have tickets scattered throughout various user accounts and not know which one to use when signing in.

To solve the problem of multiple end-user accounts for the same person, Zendesk has a feature that allows you to merge end-user accounts. When you merge these accounts, Zendesk applies the concept of a *source* and a *target* user account. The idea is that the details of the source user account will be merged into the target, and any tickets requested by the source will also be merged into the target. Once the process is complete, the source user profile will be deleted entirely and only a single user profile will remain.

The Zendesk Voice channel is a very common example of when merging users will be valuable, because often your customers will have an existing profile without a phone number. When they call your support team for assistance, a new profile will be created for the phone number from which they are calling. By merging this new user profile with an existing profile that has an email address, your agents can continue the support conversation using email.

Because Zendesk allows only a single value for some of the user profile fields (e.g., name, phone number, and time zone selection), only the values on the target user account will be retained. In the case of fields that support multiple values (e.g., email), all values will be kept from both user profiles.

To merge an end-user account, you first must find the user and view his profile. When you click the "User options" link for this user, one of the options is "Merge into another user." The dialog box to merge end-user accounts has two sections, as shown in Figure 4-2.

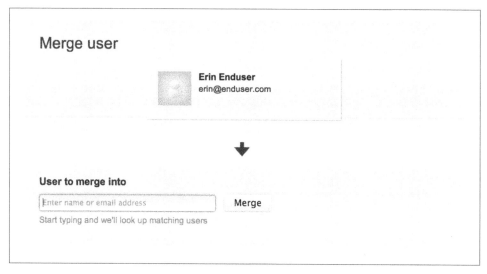

Figure 4-2. Dialog box to merge user accounts: source (top) and target (bottom)

The top section represents the source user profile and the bottom represents the target user profile. An arrow indicates this visually. To find the target user, start typing his name, and Zendesk will autopredict the user based on a text search. After you've selected the user, follow the prompts to merge the user accounts.

It's not possible to undo the process of merging users.

Suspending End Users

Occasionally, emails will get past the suspended ticket filters, or someone will sign in to your Zendesk instance and create a ticket when she really shouldn't. There are dozens of situations in which this would happen, but common examples are spam or solicitation. If this situation occurs, it's possible for you as an administrator, or your agents, to suspend that end user. If you're an administrator, you can also suspend agent accounts, though this function is used less frequently.

There are two ways to suspend a user. Outside the context of a specific ticket, you can suspend a user account by clicking the name to open the profile and then selecting the "Suspend access" option from the "User options" menu. This will suspend the user immediately without a confirmation screen. It's possible to immediately unsuspend the user by selecting the "Unsuspend access" option in the same menu.

Rather than suspending a user from her profile screen, you'll want more often to suspend a user from a specific ticket. To perform this function from a ticket screen, select the user's profile name from the navigation at the top of the page, and then select "Suspend access" from the "User options" menu. This will immediately suspend the user, which prevents her from signing in to Zendesk or submitting additional tickets via any other channel.

Assuming an End User's Profile

As you're configuring your Zendesk instance, you may periodically need to troubleshoot issues that registered end users are having using your Help Center. The "Assume identity" feature allows you to do this.

When you use this feature to assume an end user's profile, you will be signed in as that end user, and that user's view of the Help Center will be opened in a new browser tab. At the top of the Help Center, you'll see a message indicating this and a link to revert to your own identity. If you flip back to the browser tab in which you're signed in to your Zendesk instance as an administrator, you'll see a similar message. While you're assuming an end user, you cannot also access your administrator account in your Zendesk instance. It's one or the other.

Any changes you make while assuming an end user cannot be traced you, so be careful with your use of this feature. It may raise some eyebrows if an end user appears to be making comments on tickets and he has no knowledge of the comments himself.

Organizations

The Organization feature is an easy way to collect your end-user profiles together, then apply specific rules to those profiles. This particular feature is generally useful only if you're operating a business-to-business (B2B) support service, where you are aware of the organizations that you are supporting. If you are business-to-consumer (B2C) support service and you are generally unaware of your customer list, or your list of customer organizations is extremely diverse, it doesn't make as much sense to use the Organizations feature (although there are a few exceptions).

The first step to set up organizations is to visit the People administration page, and click the "organization" link next to "add" in the upper-right corner of the screen. The organization creation page has a number of fields to be completed. The Name of the organization is a required field, and would typically be the business name or brand of the organization. This name will be visible to agents when they are answering support requests. The Details and Notes fields are optional pieces of information that you can add to the organization, again for the reference of support agents.

To make it easier to link end-user accounts to organizations, Zendesk allows you to specify the email domains that are associated with that organization. The option is labeled "Domains." If you add several domain names to this field (separated by spaces), Zendesk will retroactively find all user accounts with an email addresses that matches that domain name, and automatically add the users to the organization. Whenever a new user account is created, Zendesk will also check the email address of the user against known domain names, and add them to an organization if there is a valid match.

On a basic level, organizations are useful to support agents because they will identify to which organization their ticket requester belongs. On a more advanced level, rules can be set up that will allow escalations based on certain organizations SLAs, or triage tickets automatically based on rules defined for certain organizations. Many of these examples will be explained later in this book.

Unfortunately, many customers confuse Organizations with Groups. The difference is simple. Organizations are for end users (customers), and Groups are for agents (customer service staff). End users *cannot* be added to Groups. Agents can technically be added to an Organization, but there are so few examples of where this is useful that it's definitely the exception more than the rule. One situation in which it is useful to add an Agent to an Organization is explained in "Restricting Agent Access to Tickets" on page 117.

Shared Organizations

For privacy reasons, it's generally best to restrict end users to accessing their own tickets only. In some unique situations, it might be useful to allow a person from an organization to read tickets submitted by other people at the same organization. This feature is known as *Shared Organizations*, and is useful only if you are using the Organizations feature from the previous topic.

Shared organizations can be enabled on an organization-wide basis or an individual user basis. You can enable it on an organization-wide basis by setting the Users option to "Can view all org tickets" when adding or editing the organization. This setting will immediately add a link called "Organization requests" to the "My Activities" page in the Help Center. An example of this is shown in Figure 4-3. Clicking the "Organization requests" link in the screenshot will show the tickets from other end users in this organization.

Figure 4-3. End user navigation bar, demonstrating the Organization name

 In general, we don't recommend sharing an organization unless you are completely sure that your users will not have privacy issues. It's risky to assume that an end user won't accidentally publish a credit card number or password in his ticket, or that an HR person will not publish sensitive details about an employee, which could result in other users at the same organization accessing that information.

The alternative to the organization-wide sharing setting is to allow only certain users at an organization to view tickets requested by other users at that organization. An example for this would be a situation where an organization has a primary point of contact, or a senior staff member who needs access to all tickets. This person should be trusted with sensitive information within the organization. To enable this setting on the Starter, Regular, and Plus plans, change the Access option to "Tickets from user's org" by editing the end user's profile. If the organization-wide sharing setting has been disabled, the setting on the individual user's account will override the organization-wide setting, and the end user will have full access to tickets from the organization. If the organization-wide sharing setting has been enabled, the setting on the individual end user is redundant. The same principles apply to the Enterprise plan, but the setting is an option under "What kind of tickets can this agent access?" called "Requested by users in this agent's organization" when you are defining the agent roles.

Multiple Organizations

For some time, Zendesk customers were asking for the ability to add a user to more than one organization. This feature was added in early 2014 and is available to Plus and Enterprise plan customers.

Why would you want to add users to more than one organization? Most often, your company simply has an organizational structure that allows for (or requires) your users to belong to more than one organization and you want that reflected in your Zendesk instance. For example, your users may belong to a specific business unit in your company (let's say marketing) but work on multiple products. With multiple organizations, you can create organizations for the business units and separate organizations for each product and then associate users with each organization that they belong to.

The point of organizations is that you can assign groups or specific agents to provide support to organizations based on such things as their areas of responsibility, their location, or their expertise. So using multiple organizations, you may have one group providing support to the business unit organization and another providing support to the product organization.

Multiple organizations don't mean that you can create hierarchies within a single organization. All organizations are at the same level. You just have the option of placing users into more than one.

No administrative configuration is required to use multiple organizations other than creating the list of organizations. By editing a user's profile, you can assign her to as many organizations as needed and then select the organization to be used as the default.

One of the user's organizations is the default organization, which is used if no organization has otherwise been selected. This will be the case if a user in multiple organizations sends a support request via email. An end user can mention the organization name in the body of the email message, but there's no way for that to set the Organization field in the ticket. That's when the default organization is used. When using the support request form, however, users can explicitly select the organization they want support for—so long as you make the Organization field visible on the form.

Customer Lists

Another new feature that Zendesk recently introduced is *customer lists*. You can think of these as being similar to views, in that they are dynamically generated based on a set of criteria. For views and tickets, that criteria includes data such as priority and status, whereas for customer lists, the criteria includes user-specific data such as the organization the user belongs to, the user's ID and name, the date the account was created, the custom user fields you've created, and so on.

As with views, you can create as many customer lists as you'd like and organize your customers in many different ways for many different purposes. If you're just starting out with Zendesk and don't have many users, the value of this feature may not be immediately apparent to you. However, all of the user configuration you do in your Zendesk instance now (like creating and using organizations, user and organization tags, and custom user fields) will bear fruit later when you're ready to leverage this feature.

So how might you use customer lists? You could start by creating lists of users by organization or language or tags, for example, just so that you have a quick view of those users. If you wanted a list of all the customers that have created an account in your Help Center in the last 30 days, you could do that as well. Based on a custom user field or a tag, you could create a list of all your VIP customers (Figure 4-4). These lists are useful on their own, of course, but the real value of this feature may be in the actions you take to manage these segments of customers.

Figure 4-4. An example of some of the uses of customer lists

For example, you could take the list of VIP customers you created and then load it into one of the customer engagement apps (e.g., SurveyMonkey or MailChimp) available as add-ons to your Zendesk instance. Perhaps you want to run an email campaign offering your VIP customers a special discount on a new product or service. Loading your list into MailChimp makes that easy to do. You can also export a list as a CSV file and use it in an application outside of your Zendesk instance.

This feature is available in the Regular, Plus, and Enterprise plans, where you'll find it in the side toolbar just below Views. Both administrators and agents can use this feature, with the caveat that agents can create lists only for their own use (personal lists) whereas administrators can create personal lists, lists that a specific group can see, and lists that all agents can see. Only administrators can install the MailChimp and SurveyMonkey apps in Zendesk, but agents can use those apps to create email campaigns or surveys from customer lists if you allow them access to these apps. When you install these apps, you can set role restrictions if you want to prevent agents from using them, which is probably a good idea if you want to control communications with your customers.

In the Enterprise version of Zendesk, as mentioned earlier in "Configuration Options for Agent Roles" on page 44, you can restrict agents to just see customer lists but not create them, or you can allow them to create personal, group, or global customer lists.

CHAPTER 5

Channels

There are nine different ways in which a ticket can be added to Zendesk, each of which is defined as a *channel*. Some of the channels, such as the Help Center and email, are so common that almost every organization uses them. Other channels, such as chat or the Feedback Tab, would probably be used more frequently if customers were aware of them. The Voice channel is the only channel that has an extra cost associated with it. The Facebook and Twitter channels are probably best suited to organizations with a certain social media awareness (although we'll expand on this in "Twitter" on page 69). The Ticket Sharing channel is an advanced feature used to integrate several Zendesk systems, or Zendesk with other software platforms. The final channel, the application programming interface (API), is a way of programmatically connecting Zendesk with other software systems, or adding new tickets into the system without direct user intervention. Technically speaking, tickets created using the mobile applications are created using the API, though we generally consider them in the same category as tickets created via the Help Center.

According to a study, 58% of online retail customers prefer email as their medium for customer support, 22% prefer phone, and 20% prefer chat. These metrics might provide some useful context to what is most important to your customers, and further details of the study are available from the full infographic (*http://bit.ly/cust-support*).

Zendesk includes multiple channels because you should be able to provide support to your customers in as many different ways as possible. Every person will be more comfortable contacting your customer service team using one specific channel, and providing that person with the option to use this channel is the first step in creating a great support experience. For this reason, we encourage all Zendesk customers to leverage every possible channel. With a small amount of setup by administrators and education on behalf of your agents, you should be able to support all of these channels without any difficulty.

This chapter does not include the Help Center channel because some of the important concepts have already been covered in "Help Center Branding" on page 12, "Customizing the Zendesk URL" on page 13, and "Internationalization" on page 15, and it's covered in depth in Chapter 9.

The Zendesk API channel is not covered in the current version of this book, though you can visit the Zendesk Developer Portal (*http://developer.zendesk.com/*) for more information about programmatically interfacing with your Zendesk instance.

Incoming Email

Email is probably the most frequently used channel in Zendesk, for the simple reason that most people are already familiar with it. The benefit of email to customers is that it's easy for them to assume that the *support@* prefix on your corporate domain name is going to connect with your support team somehow. This is also less effort for your customers than if they were to visit your website, navigate to the support section, and fill out the potentially extensive set of mandatory fields that you've added to your Zendesk instance (we'll discuss why it's not a good idea to have too many required fields on page 90). The beauty of email is that it's also universal, and a very effective bidirectional channel of communication. Zendesk relies on communicating with users via outgoing emails as much as it relies on email as an incoming communication channel.

Adding Incoming Email Addresses

When you create your Zendesk instance, you'll select a subdomain that is relevant to your company name (see "Customizing the Zendesk URL" on page 13 for more information). In my fictional company "Blue Skies," my subdomain is *blueskies* and my Zendesk URL is *blueskies.zendesk.com*. Immediately after I've created this Zendesk instance, emails sent to the *support@blueskies.zendesk.com* email address will be created as new tickets in Zendesk. In addition, emails sent to the *sales@blueskies.zendesk.com* and *members@blueskies.zendesk.com* email addresses will be created as tickets. It doesn't matter which email prefix is used, because any email that is sent to the *@blueskies.zendesk.com* email address suffix (based on the domain name) will create a new ticket in Zendesk. The broad scope of incoming email addresses might sound like there is a risk of spam entering Zendesk, but the suspended tickets feature (covered on page 28) will take care of this for you.

If you elect to use several email addresses, such as *support@blueskies.com*, *sales@blueskies.com*, and *members@blueskies.com*, your mail server administrators should set up three forwarding rules. The process to set up a custom domain with forwarding is described in "Customizing the Email Domain" on page 21. Each rule should forward one email address to the relevant email address inside Zendesk. If you leverage the ability to have multiple incoming email addresses, it also adds a lot of value as an automatic triage tool. An example of this is provided in "Trigger Examples" on page 135.

Most of the incoming email channel settings are changed outside of Zendesk, and the Email section inside the Channels administration page is dedicated mostly to outgoing emails instead.

Agent Forwarding

It's not uncommon to find that some support agents provide such a high level of customer service that their customers seek out their direct email address and start emailing them directly to request support. Unfortunately, this causes a number of problems. The first problem is that support requests answered in email don't have all of the benefits of requests submitted via the usual Zendesk channels. Another problem is that your superstar support agent might not be working that day, so any requests sent directly to that agent via email will go unnoticed. Even if the agent *is* working that day, she probably doesn't want a barrage of emails sent to her, and would prefer to be delegated requests at the same rate as all other agents on the customer service team.

To make it as easy as possible to take the support conversation out of email and redirect it into Zendesk, the product has a feature named *agent forwarding*. This feature allows an agent who receives a support request directly via email to forward that request (by clicking the Forward button in her email application) into Zendesk. Zendesk will receive the request and detect that the sender of this email is an agent. It will understand that the agent is submitting a ticket on behalf of a customer, and will start to read the contents of the email to find the name of the original sender. When it finds a section of text that says "From:" with a name and email address, it will create a new profile (or use an existing profile) for that user, and create the ticket as if it was submitted by him directly.

All that is required for an agent to use this feature is to forward emails to the standard incoming support email address. In the examples we've been using, the agent would forward the email from her customer to *support@blueskies.com*. From an administrator's perspective, this feature must be enabled before it can be used. By default, this setting is disabled in Zendesk. To enable it, open the Agents administration page and check the option to "Enable email forwarding."

Voice

The Zendesk Voice channel adds call center capabilities to your Zendesk instance, via the Twilio platform. The best part of this feature is that it's seamlessly integrated into Zendesk, which means that incoming calls will be immediately matched to existing end-user accounts, and those end users will be able to listen to a recording of the conversation after the call has ended. The support conversation can continue via comments and emails, and the full record of the initial conversation is easily available within the support request.

Voice is the only channel that has an additional cost in Zendesk, which is due to Zendesk's partnering with Twilio, a separate paid offering, to provide the service. At the time of writing, the cost of this service per minute for incoming calls varies based on the country and whether your agents answer calls in a web browser or using a telephone. There are additional fees associated with other features such as forwarding to cell phones and landlines, and voicemail transcription to text. Full details of pricing are available from the Zendesk Voice pricing page (*http://bit.ly/zd-voice*).

Adding Phone Numbers

To get started with Zendesk Voice, you'll need to set up a phone number on which to receive incoming calls. This phone number can be a local number with a specified area code for your location, or a national toll-free number in the US, Canada, or the UK. You can also elect to have several phone numbers configured for Zendesk Voice, or phone numbers in many different countries. At the time of writing, Zendesk Voice supports phone numbers in the US, Canada, and the UK, plus 12 other European countries and 4 countries in the Asia Pacific region. In the near future, Zendesk will add support for most countries around the world.

To add a phone number, open the Voice section inside the Channels administration page. Before any of the Voice administration tabs appear, you must create at least one phone number. The first step when creating a number is to select the country; then, you will have the option of entering a few digits into the phone number search field, which will narrow the results to include only phone numbers that contain those digits. Some organizations like to select phone numbers in a certain regional area, or numbers that match existing phone number patterns for their organization. It's also possible to select a number based on a text phrase.

Publishing Your Voice Phone Number

For some organizations, the choice of Zendesk Voice phone number does not matter very much, because they will be forwarding an existing phone number (often a national toll-free number) to the new number set up in Zendesk Voice. The immediate benefit of taking this route is that there's no need to distribute a new phone number to your customers, because you can use your existing phone number. The potential downside is that there may be a cost for this service, which you'll need to confirm with your phone provider.

If your existing support phone number has an answering service with a selection process like "Press 1 for Sales, 2 for Support," you should forward customers who press 2 to the new phone number you've set up inside Zendesk.

The other benefit of keeping your existing phone number and routing it to Zendesk is that it makes it easier to migrate away from Zendesk Voice at a later time if it becomes necessary. It's currently possible to port your number in and out of Zendesk Voice if you're in the US, but in other countries the Voice number is not currently transferrable, so having a phone number independent of any customer service tool gives you the most flexibility, similar to the way that your URL can be configured to be transferrable in "Customizing the Zendesk URL" on page 13.

After finding a number that you're happy with, click "Choose number," then "Purchase this number," after reading the terms and conditions. Immediately after confirming the number, you can publish the new phone number to customers and they can call your customer service portal on this number. When a customer calls, Zendesk Voice uses a round-robin system to direct the call to the agent who has been waiting the longest to receive the call. The agent will have 30 seconds to accept the call before it is passed on to the next agent in line.

After you've created at least one phone number, the Voice channel administration page will change to include several tabs, each of which serves a purpose for administration of the Voice channel. The Numbers tab will contain a list of the numbers added, and you may visit it at any point to change the settings for your Voice phone numbers.

It is not currently possible to forward incoming calls to certain agents directly, based on specified criteria. For example, a common request is that all calls to a Canadian Zendesk Voice phone number should be directed to agents in Canada, whereas calls to a UK phone number should be directed to support agents in the UK. It's also not possible at this time to transfer incoming calls between agents, and it's not possible to make outgoing calls. All of these feature requests are on the radar of the Zendesk product management team.

Call Center Configuration

After you've set up the incoming phone numbers for your Zendesk instance, you'll also need to select the options to determine how the call center operates. Most of the options on the General Settings tab on the Voice channel administration page are intuitive, but we'll focus on a couple of them in this section.

First, you need to make a decision about how many callers should be waiting in the queue before redirecting new callers to voicemail. This option has a maximum of 15, so it's impossible for you to determine that all callers, regardless of the length of the queue, should wait in line. The default option is 5. The other option associated with the queue size is the queue wait time. This option checks the length of the wait of each caller in the queue, and any caller who has exceeded the specified time limit will be forwarded to voicemail. The purpose of this option is to impose a hard limit on the level of frustration your users may experience waiting to speak to a customer service representative.

The maximum wait allowed by Zendesk is 20 minutes and the default is 1 minute. As I explained in "Adding Phone Numbers" on page 60, incoming calls will alert an agent for exactly 30 seconds before being forwarded to the next waiting agent. Therefore, a maximum wait time of 1 minute will give only two support agents the opportunity to accept the call, but will relieve the frustration of the person calling your support team, because after 1 minute he will be redirected to voicemail and have an opportunity to leave a message to be contacted by a member of your support team.

The other important option on the Voice administration page is the "New live call recordings are public?" option. We really like the idea that calls to your customer service team are not only recorded for agents to review, but also recorded for the caller to review. The level of transparency offered to customers by this option will likely be far more common in the future, and I encourage you to use it. The default option is that recordings are "public," meaning that end users can listen to them. If you are uncomfortable with this option and prefer for your customers not to be able to hear the recordings of their calls, then you can set this option to "No," which means that the recordings are private. There is no option to disable recordings completely.

 If you are an administrator and also the account owner for your Zendesk instance, you can configure a voicemail transcription service, which has an extra cost of 5 cents per minute (at the time of writing). It currently only supports the English language, and can be used on voicemails only (i.e., this feature does not transcribe all incoming calls). This feature is enabled automatically for English language instances using Zendesk Voice, but if you'd like to disable it, you can change the settings from the Subscription tab on the Account administration page.

Recording Greetings

The Zendesk Voice greeting is the first thing that customers who call your organization will hear, so make it professional and as friendly as possible. Fortunately, the Voice service has some default greetings, which feature a female voice and some soothing music that is played while customers are holding for a representative. Most of the time, these greetings will be sufficient. The voice has an American accent, so international customers may want to change the default greetings. To change the greetings, open the Greetings tab in the Voice channel administration page.

There are two ways to submit a custom greeting using the administrator portal: upload a file in MP3 format, or instruct Zendesk Voice to call your phone to record your own voice as the new greeting. The MP3 option is probably the most reliable, and has a better chance of avoiding background noise. If you're not able to create an MP3 or you'd like to get something set up quickly (but you're not happy with the defaults), select the

"Record using a phone" option and prepare your best telephone operator voice, because Zendesk Voice will call you immediately and prompt you to record the greeting.

For legal reasons, the "Available agents greeting" should always mention to the customer that the call will be recorded. The default greeting states the following message, and if you are going to record your own greeting, it's usually best to emulate this spiel:

> *Please hold while we find an available support agent to assist you. Your call may be recorded for monitoring purposes. If you would like to leave a voicemail, you may dial 1 at any time.*

Call Activity Dashboard

The Call Activity Dashboard is a tool that allows administrators to view metrics on incoming calls on Zendesk Voice. It also allows administrators to monitor the activity of agents using Zendesk Voice. You can find this dashboard by opening the Call Activity tab on the Voice administration page, and most of the values on this page, such as Calls Waiting and Average Wait Time, are intuitive. Aside from these metrics, it's also useful to scroll down this page to find out how many of your agents are actively marking themselves as being available to take calls. You can also find a report of the total number of hours in the past 24 hours that agents have marked themselves as available to take calls. If you find that your agents are not marking themselves as available as often as you'd like, this dashboard can be used as a reminder to your agents about the benefits of providing phone support to customers.

The status options listed on the call activity dashboard are:

Available
    Agent has marked himself as being available to take calls.

Not Available
    Agent is not online, or has not marked himself as available to take calls.

On Call
    Agent is currently on a support call.

Wrap Up
    Agent has just finished a call, and is making notes on the support ticket before taking more calls.

Feedback Tab

The *Feedback Tab* is probably our personal favorite incoming channel. It takes the same form that users complete to submit a support ticket on your Help Center, and adds the form to any other website of your choice. It's a way of bringing the support link directly to your customers. Not only that, but it also allows customers to submit a ticket in the context of something else that they're doing on your website, then continue browsing the website after the request has been submitted. The alternative methods of submitting a ticket—such as sending an email or visiting your Help Center—would almost certainly take customers out of the context of the task they were already performing.

An example use of a Feedback Tab is on the Zen U website (*http://universi ty.zendesk.com*). This site lists the details of training courses, and the schedule on which they are delivered. A Feedback Tab named Questions has been added to the lefthand side of every page on the website. If a customer is browsing the site and has a question about one of the courses, or the schedule, she can click the Questions button, enter in a few personal details and the description of her inquiry, and then submit the form. Afterward, she'll be immediately returned to the page on the Zen U website that she was viewing before submitting the inquiry. From the Zendesk side, a new ticket will be received in the Zendesk instance, with a note that indicates the specific web page from which the customer submitted the question. This gives some context for the inquiry, and the team members can answer the ticket like any other support ticket.

If your organization has leveraged the Help Center in Zendesk (see Chapter 9), the other great feature about the Feedback Tab is that it can provide self-service support to your customers via searching your knowledge base. Ideally, one of the articles in your knowledge base would answer the customer's question and the customer will no longer need to submit her support request and wait for a response. The options to configure this aspect of the Feedback Tab will be explained shortly, and the feature in general is only valuable if you're using the Help Center.

 If you have disabled public creation of user profiles by following the instructions in "Public Creation of User Profiles" on page 29, the Feedback Tab channel cannot be used. The technical reason is that the Feedback Tab relies on customers being able to create a user profile while submitting a ticket, but the browser cookie used to recognize a signed-in user in Zendesk cannot be accessed by an external website for security reasons.

Creating a New Feedback Tab

To get this feature working, visit the Feedback Tab section on the Channels administration page. A form on this page asks for the parameters of the Feedback Tab, including the name, color, positioning, and some other options. The option "Knowledge Base Search and Topic Suggestions" is probably the most important one on this page, because it will determine the customer's workflow to submit a ticket. If you're actively using the Forums feature inside Zendesk and you feel like your forum articles should be the first port of call for your customers, you should enable the "Enable Topic Suggestions & Knowledge Base Search" option. This option will match keywords in the customer's question with keywords in knowledge base articles, and suggest a possible answer based on the likelihood of a match. If you don't have relevant articles in your knowledge base, no results will be displayed and the support ticket can be submitted from the Feedback Tab.

Another option on this page is whether the chatting feature (covered on page 67) is enabled or disabled on the Feedback Tab. Allowing customers to chat from a Feedback Tab is a good idea if you're actively using chat, because it allows them to get immediate assistance and answers.

It's also important that you indicate whether you'd like for your custom fields to be displayed in the Feedback Tab. The option is labeled "Display custom fields to end users?" and the default is No, but we recommend setting this to Yes. Our logic is simple: if you're asking users to complete a certain set of custom fields when they create a ticket on your Help Center, there's no reason that you shouldn't ask for the same information when a ticket is submitted from a different channel. Because the Feedback Tab is considered an extension of the Help Center that you can add to your website, we recommend enabling this option so that the user experience is consistent. The only caveat is that if you've created a cascading list of options in a drop-down list (as described in "Custom Fields" on page 104), the menu will be flattened and shown to the user with the : : syntax included in each option. It's not really a big problem, but it does look a little strange.

Before you submit the Feedback Tab configuration form, be sure to visit the second tab, named Advanced Customization, and confirm whether you want to change any of the words on your Feedback Tab. You can also use Cascading Style Sheet (CSS) technology to customize the appearance of your Feedback Tab. This is typically useful if you'd like the format of your Feedback Tab to match the look and feel of your existing website.

 It's not currently possible for users to submit attachments on tickets submitted via the Feedback Tab, but those users can always visit your Help Center directly to submit a ticket, and if the attachments are enabled, they can submit attachments with that ticket. You do, however, have the option of enabling Screenr and allowing users to record and embed a screencast in a Feedback Tab support request.

An example of an open Feedback Tab—based on the default Zendesk settings—is shown in Figure 5-1.

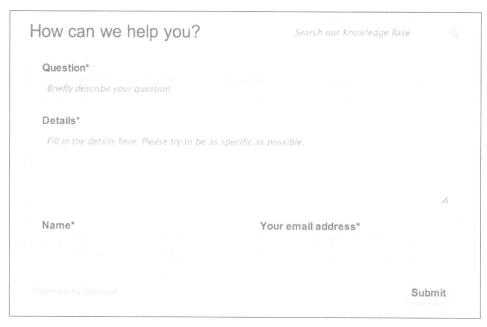

Figure 5-1. Default Feedback Tab shown to the customer

Publishing a Feedback Tab

Once you've filled out the form to create your Feedback Tab, you can click "Preview & grab code snippet," and Zendesk will take you to another page that has a small piece of JavaScript code, similar to the following:

```
<script type="text/javascript"
  src="//assets.zendesk.com/external/zenbox/v2.5/zenbox.js"></script>
<style type="text/css" media="screen, projection">
  @import url(//assets.zendesk.com/external/zenbox/v2.5/zenbox.css);
</style>
<script type="text/javascript">
  if (typeof(Zenbox) !== "undefined") {
    Zenbox.init({
      dropboxID:   "20079071",
      url:         "https://yourcompanyname.zendesk.com",
      tabID:       "Support",
      tabColor:    "black",
      tabPosition: "Left"
    });
  }
</script>
```

You don't need to be an HTML or JavaScript expert to use the Feedback Tab. You just need to copy and paste this JavaScript into an email addressed to your webmaster, with instructions to add the JavaScript immediately before the </body> tag on the website where you'd like the Feedback Tab to appear. The webmaster will do the rest, and the next time you visit your website, you'll find a button similar to the one on *university.zendesk.com*.

Managing Existing Feedback Tabs

After you complete the process defined in "Creating a New Feedback Tab" on page 64, a new Feedback Tab will be created with a unique ID. If you open the Feedback Tab administration section in Zendesk again tomorrow, you'll find that the settings have been returned to the defaults, and you'll need to customize them again and submit the form to get a new Feedback Tab ID. The fact that each new submission creates a new tab is a good thing, because it allows you to create many different Feedback Tabs with many different settings. You might like to have a whole set of Feedback Tabs depending on the language selection of visitors to your website, or many Feedback Tabs with different labels on the fields presented to the user.

 Using the administrator portal, you can't currently find previously defined Feedback Tabs and edit their settings. Fortunately, if you're savvy and can follow the instructions in this section, it's not difficult to do this manually.

Of course, if you want to just change a single option on an existing Feedback Tab, it would be a lot of effort to reconfigure all options entirely just to achieve this. If you've ever created or edited a Feedback Tab, you may have noticed that the URL contains the unique ID of that Tab. If you visit the URL */account/dropboxes/uniqueFeebackTabID/edit* on your Zendesk instance, replacing *uniqueFeebackTabID* with the unique ID of your own Feedback Tab, you'll be able to update the existing Feedback Tab settings by submitting the form again. To find this ID, check the source code of your website hosting the existing Feedback Tab, and look for the number following `dropboxID:`.

At some point in the future, it may be possible to use the web interface to edit existing Feedback Tabs, and Zendesk may change the behavior so that it's not possible to perform the steps listed in this section. For the moment, though, this is a neat trick that will save you time and effort when editing existing Tabs.

Chatting

The ability to chat in Zendesk is a feature that provides real-time support to your customers, without adding a significant burden to your agents. It is the only channel that is not available on the Starter plan. The common misconception about the chat channel is that if it's enabled, you must chain your agents to their desks so they are available to your customers every minute of the day. This is not really an accurate assumption, because Zendesk deals very well with situations when no agents are available to accept a chat request. If this occurs, the customer is simply informed that an agent is not currently available to answer the request, and is prompted to submit a ticket using a different method.

Setting Up Chat

The chat channel is disabled by default in Zendesk. If you want to use it, enable it from the Chat section of the Channels administration page. The first option on the Chat administration page is the option to enable or disable chat entirely. On this page you'll also have the option to modify the welcome message, if you'd like to welcome your customers with something other than the default, which is:

> Hi there. How can I help today?

It's rare to change the chat message because the default is so generic, but we did once train a very enthusiastic organization that changed the chat message to include several smiley faces and exclamation marks.

The other option on this page, "Maximum chat requests per agent," has a dual purpose. The first purpose is to prevent an agent from trying to accept more chats than she can handle. This will prevent context switching that might result in incorrect information being provided to a customer. The other purpose, and probably the most important, is to identify the maximum number of requests that can be handled in your entire Zendesk instance. For example, if you have set the maximum chat requests to 2 per agent, and 5 agents have signed into chat, your Zendesk instance can handle 10 active chat conversations in parallel. Once your agents reach the total limit, the "chat about this ticket" link will disappear entirely from the end users' ticket screen. This is a simple way to manage expectations with your customers.

Chatting from a Ticket Versus a Feedback Tab

When we refer to the chat function in Zendesk, we're really talking about two different features. The first feature is the "chat about my ticket" function. This function is enabled only if the option is selected in the Chat administration page. When this feature is enabled and if an agent is available to chat, the Chat window will appear in the Help Center and the end user can click it to begin a chat session. It basically gives customers the ability to quickly seek help on their ticket, while they're already in the context of the support request. This chat function is used exclusively for existing tickets.

The other chat function is used exclusively to create new tickets, and is available only from the Feedback Tab. As noted on page 63, the Feedback Tab—and implicitly the ability for customers to chat from the Feedback Tab—will be available only if you've enabled public creation of user profiles on your Zendesk instance. Refer back to "Public Creation of User Profiles" on page 29 for details on how to do this. If you have chat enabled in your Zendesk instance, you'll see the option "End users can chat with agents?" on the configuration form to create a Feedback Tab. If this is set to Yes, the Feedback Tab workflow will include a new step (shown in Figure 5-2) that asks the user whether he would like to chat immediately or submit a new ticket instead. If the customer elects to chat with an agent, the resulting chat conversation will be created as a new ticket, and the customer will have access to the entire conversation afterward.

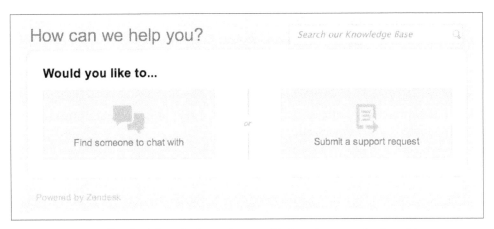

Figure 5-2. A Feedback Tab with the option enabled to chat or submit a ticket

In "Setting Up Chat" on page 68, we explained that the chat function disappears from the end-user interface when no agents are currently available to chat. The Feedback Tab is quite different: even if there are no agents available, the chat option will always be displayed in a Feedback Tab if the chat option is enabled for that Feedback Tab. The reason is that Zendesk will not make a query back to the Zendesk servers when a Feedback Tab is opened to validate that an agent is available to chat. It is only after the user elects to chat with an agent that the Feedback Tab will check agent availability, then politely inform the customer if an agent is not available. If the chat cannot proceed, the user is always encouraged to complete the process of submitting her ticket to your customer service team using the standard Feedback Tab form.

Twitter

We mentioned earlier in this chapter that Twitter is a channel suited for organizations that have an active social media presence. Actually, this does a small disservice to the Twitter channel. A more accurate description would be to say that the Twitter channel is useful for companies whose *customers* have a social media presence. It doesn't matter quite as much whether your own company is on Twitter, because the purpose of the Twitter channel is to find what your customers are talking about, and if they're talking about your organization, you can take those conversations and turn them into actionable tickets inside your Zendesk instance.

According to Micah Solomon, "Twitter and other social media tools *do* have the power to bring about regime change in the business world." According to a study on the use of social media for support, 62% of all consumers have used social media for customer service issues (see the full infographic (*http://bit.ly/smedia-sup*)). Another study on Twitter found that 19% of all consumers use Twitter on a monthly basis for the specific purpose of seeking customer service (the full infographic (*http://bit.ly/zen-twitter*) has more details). A study by ISMDealers (*http://bit.ly/ismdealers*) identified that 58% of the people who tweeted about a bad customer service issue expected a response from the target company, but according to another study (*http://bit.ly/keep-twitter*), only 13% of complaints received a response.

The implication is clear: Twitter should be considered a key piece in the customer service strategy adopted by any organization.

 Before getting started, here's a piece of trivia that usually makes people laugh: when you convert a "tweet" into a "ticket" in Zendesk, it's called a "twicket." It's a funny portmanteau, but twickets themselves should be taken seriously. They're a big deal because comments added to twickets will be automatically tweeted back to the whole world. For a support agent who isn't expecting this, it can be quite a surprise when he writes something perhaps not suited for the Twittersphere. It's important that your agents are aware of the difference between a *ticket* and a *twicket*—it's more than a *w*.

Selecting a Twitter Handle for Zendesk

Before you can start using Twitter inside Zendesk, you must create a Twitter handle via the Twitter website. Most organizations have a corporate Twitter handle already, which is probably named after their brand. For example, Wells Fargo Bank in America has the Twitter handle @WellsFargo. Generally, I don't recommend using this corporate Twitter handle to respond to tweets from Zendesk. There are a few reasons for this:

Risk of mistakes
Your biggest risk on Twitter (whether or not you're using Zendesk) is that someone will post an inappropriate tweet and the whole world will read it. In Zendesk, where there are many ways in which to post information to the world via Twitter, this risk increases.

Focus
Should the focus of your corporate Twitter handle be on exciting news about your organization and links to useful information for your customers, or individual re-

sponses to support requests? Most people would say the former. While you have the podium, we advise you to use it for the highest valued purpose.

Noise pollution

If you're offering support to your customers via Twitter, you might find that your Twitter handle starts to contain so many support requests that it's common for customers to tune out. It's never a good thing if your customers tune out of your primary Twitter presence entirely.

For this reason, Wells Fargo Bank also created the @Ask_WellsFargo Twitter handle. In fact, we discovered this handle in 2009 when the company responded to a tweet one of us had posted after an exceptional customer service experience at a local bank branch. The Twitter response made a lasting impression, and illustrates the potential value of using the Twitter channel to support your customers.

On the other side of the coin, it's worth noting that Zendesk itself uses its corporate Twitter handle @Zendesk (*http://www.twitter.com/@Zendesk*) for all responses related to support requests. That's a conscious decision the company made by weighing the factors just explained.

Authorizing a Twitter Handle

To authorize a Twitter handle, visit the Twitter section of the Channels administration page in Zendesk. The "Twitter accounts" tab allows you to authorize Zendesk access to Twitter accounts. If you have multiple corporate identities and would like to give your agents the option to tweet from a different one occasionally, you can set up multiple handles. Otherwise, one authorized Twitter handle is usually enough. Authorization of the Twitter handle uses the industry standard OAuth authentication protocol, which means that even when you authorize the Twitter account, Zendesk will never have access to your Twitter password. The list of permissions requested by Twitter is shown in Figure 5-3.

After you authorize a Twitter handle and you are returned to the Zendesk administration portal, click the "edit" link for that handle. There are four settings on this page that are important for you to configure immediately. The Primary option will determine whether this is the account from which all Zendesk tweets should originate. The "Capture incoming direct messages as tickets" option is useful only if you expect your customers to Direct Message (DM) you on Twitter. The "Track favorites" option simply means that all favorited tweets on Twitter will be automatically added as new tickets in Zendesk.

 The "Track favorites" option is enabled by default, and we usually recommend that you disable it, unless you're sure that you'll be using the favorites feature of Twitter for this purpose. If your social media team is using favorites in Twitter for another purpose, this option will cause twickets to be created unnecessarily.

Figure 5-3. Authentication screen for Twitter

Finally, the "Capture public mentions as tickets" option can be used to ensure that all mentions of the authorized Twitter handle in tweets are automatically converted into twickets. When deciding whether to enable this option, you should take two considerations into account:

Percentage of complaints

If you're a company with such a strong reputation that the vast majority of your customers who mention your organization on Twitter are praising you, it's not going to be worth your time to have all of those tweets converted into tickets automatically. You'll spend more time closing out unnecessary twickets than replying to the valid ones.

Volume

If you find that, on average, you get only 50 mentions of your Twitter handle per day, it might be OK to convert all of them into twickets automatically and then triage them as necessary. If you find that you get 5,000 mentions of your Twitter handle per day, however, it might be a lot less manageable. Decide whether to process your tweets automatically or manually based on the number of tweets that you can reasonably process in a day.

Linking Tweets into Zendesk

When one of your agents adds a comment to a twicket in Zendesk, she will have the option to tweet that comment to the requester, and continue the conversation. The agent may like to continue the conversation on Twitter—in which case, she would choose not to provide a link to the ticket in Zendesk—or she might like to encourage the requester to sign into the Help Center to continue the conversation and solve the support request.

As an administrator, you have some control over the way that links in your outgoing tweets are configured. By default, Zendesk uses the bit.ly URL shortening service to shorten the full URL of the Zendesk ticket into a shortened URL. There are many URL shortening services that allow you to measure metrics on the number of visitors to your links, and of this list, Zendesk supports bit.ly, ow.ly, and is.gd. To use one of these services, you must first sign up with an account on that service, then select the correct option from the list in Zendesk and enter your relevant credentials for that service. We recommend that you enable one of these URL shortening services, because most of them measure the number of visitors who click the relevant links, which helps you to understand the traction that you're getting with your customer service tweets. You should create a dedicated account with the URL shortening service for this purpose; otherwise, the overall visitor metrics may be polluted by other shortened URLs not related to Zendesk.

If you prefer to tweet to customers but not to continue the conversations inside Zendesk, you can disable the "Append ticket links to outgoing tweets?" option entirely. Alternatively, you can enable agents to make this decision on a case-by-case basis. There is a checkbox labeled "Always include shortened ticket URL" on the Twitter settings page, but we think that this option is confusing. What it's essentially saying is "Do you want to give agents the option to include a link to the ticket in the tweet?" We like this option because it gives control to the agent. If your customer tweets, "I can't log into your website," the proper agent response is to reply to the twicket and include a link to continue the conversation in Zendesk. If another customer tweets, "The colors on your website are too dark," an agent can respond to notify the person that the comment has been received, but elect not to provide a link to continue the conversation, which does not necessarily warrant further dialog inside Zendesk.

We highly recommend that your agents take the Twitter conversation into the Zendesk agent interface as quickly as possible, and solve the support ticket more privately. Twitter's 140-character limit is very restrictive for communicating on a support request, but the bigger problem is that Twitter is a public platform, and it's often difficult to solve a support request without providing at least some personal information. There are also other benefits of moving the conversation into the Zendesk agent interface, such as reducing the noise on your Twitter stream, preserving the conversation for future reference, and attaching files more conveniently.

Saved Searches

Authorizing a Twitter handle with Zendesk and selecting the options listed in the previous sections is really just the first step to using Twitter. Unless you've selected the option to automatically capture public mentions as tickets, no twickets will be created in your Zendesk instance. If you'd like to have more control over the twicket creation process, you will need to create *Twitter Saved Searches*. Saved searches allow administrators to define specific keywords that will be monitored by agents in Zendesk. There are certain keywords that we always encourage Zendesk administrators to monitor:

Your corporate Twitter handle(s)
> In the Wells Fargo example, this rule would include @WellsFargo and @Ask_WellsFargo (two separate saved searches). The purpose of these searches is to find all users who are tweeting something directly to you. Here's a trick for this one: if you create a search for @WellsFargo, you'll see all tweets that mention this Twitter handle, but also all tweets *from* this Twitter handle in the search results. To avoid this, you can write your search query as "to:WellsFargo" without the quotation marks (and replacing "WellsFargo" with your corporate Twitter handle). This syntax in Twitter will include only tweets *to* your organization and exclude the ones *from* it, and you'll have slightly fewer tweets to read before finding the ones you care about.

Your brand names
> Sometimes customers don't tweet to @WellsFargo, but tweet or mention "Wells Fargo" instead. It's a good idea to create a separate saved search for your company name, and even common misspellings of your company name. All of these saved searches will increase the likelihood that you'll catch a comment from a customer who is expressing some sort of dissatisfaction with your company, which is an opportunity for you to satisfy the customer with the help of your excellent customer service team.

After you've created these saved searches, they will appear on the Manage Searches tab of the Twitter Settings administration page. You then click on the tweets listed in the search results, convert the tweets to twickets, and start the conversation with the customer.

Facebook

Unlike Twitter, the Facebook channel is really useful only if you have an active social presence on Facebook. The reason is that this integration relies on your organization having a Facebook page, which is similar to a Facebook personal profile, but is set up for a company or brand instead of a person. This integration will allow you to automatically take all posts on the timeline of the Facebook page, or messages sent privately to the Facebook page, and create them as new tickets inside Zendesk. Your agents will be able to respond to the tickets, and comments will be automatically posted back to the Facebook timeline, or added to the private message conversation.

An interesting Facebook metric appears in a study by ISMDealers (*http://bit.ly/ismdeal ers*), which finds that "46% of Facebook users say they would talk about or recommend a product on Facebook." This means that if you're not leveraging this channel in Zendesk, there is a risk that you're missing a lot of conversations about your product or brand. Some of these people posting might be open to a conversation with your customer service team, improving the social perception of your organization.

 When you take a Facebook post and create a ticket, it's not called a "ficket" for obvious reasons.

Authorizing the App

To set up the Facebook channel, visit the Facebook section of the Channels administration page. From this page, click the "Add your first Facebook page" link. Unfortunately, there's one aspect of the Facebook integration that is a little bit unusual: in order to sign into Facebook, you must have a personal profile. Facebook pages can exist on their own, but the way that Zendesk accesses a Facebook page is by going through an authorized Facebook personal profile. This means that the user with administrative access to the relevant Facebook page will need to enter her Facebook username and password and add the app (shown in Figure 5-4), then authorize all permissions for the Facebook app (shown in Figure 5-5) to access the Facebook page on her behalf. The good news is that this authorization needs to be done only once.

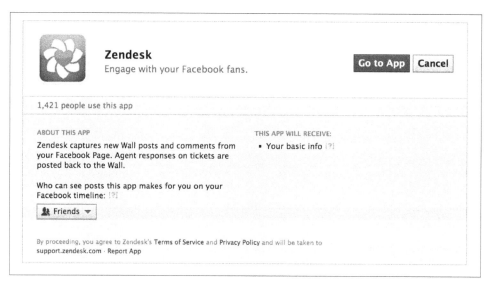

Figure 5-4. Facebook confirmation to add the Zendesk app

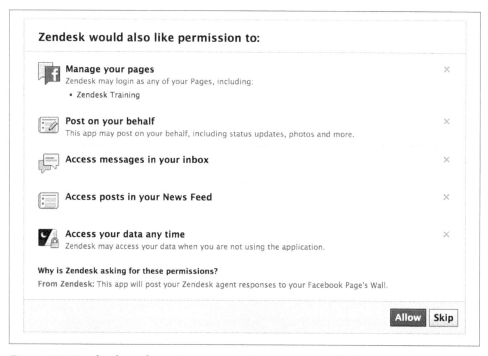

Figure 5-5. Facebook confirmation to authorize permissions for the app

When that process is complete and the Zendesk app is authorized by the Facebook user, Zendesk is able to access the Facebook pages to which that user has administrative access.

Monitoring Posts and Messages

Users on the Regular, Plus, and Enterprise plans are allowed to authorize two Facebook pages in Zendesk, and users on the Starter plan can authorize one page only.

After you've authorized the app, Zendesk will list the Facebook pages to which the authorized user has administrative access. For each one of these pages, the list of options shown in Figure 5-6 will be presented, with the default selections shown in the figure. If you'd like to hit the ground running and import recent activity in the past week from your Facebook page, select the third option, "Import recent activity." After you've selected your options, click the Add button. The page will be linked immediately and new posts will be created as tickets. When this process is complete, the Facebook page will never need to be authorized within Zendesk again.

Figure 5-6. Options when linking a Facebook page for monitoring

You can change options later. For example, you might discover that most of the posts on the *timeline* of the Facebook page are supportive and not related to support, but that the Facebook *messages* are predominantly used for customer service inquiries. To change these settings, navigate to the Facebook channel administration page and click the "edit" link beside the name of the page.

If you're collecting wall posts from your Facebook page, there is an option for you to "Include Wall posts authored by the Page." This option will determine whether posts that were authored by the page itself should be copied into Zendesk as new tickets. At first glance, it might seem like this option should be disabled because the posts made by members of your own team will never be requests for support. Actually, it's the comments on this post that are important to capture, and enabling this option will allow you to do this. So it's recommended that you leave this option enabled (which it is by default).

 It's possible to selectively convert tweets into twickets using Twitter, but currently it's not possible to selectively take posts from the timeline of the Facebook page and add them into Zendesk. The simple reason for the difference is that the Facebook API is a lot more restrictive than the Twitter API, and doesn't have the same mechanisms that Zendesk uses for the Twitter functionality. The Facebook integration currently draws every post from the timeline into Zendesk, regardless of the subject matter.

In "Default Automations" on page 141, we describe an automation that will close tickets from Twitter and Facebook one day after the ticket is solved, and we also explain the reasons why this is important.

Eight Reasons to Monitor Social Media

Not every organization currently has a social media presence, and not every organization needs one. But social media is growing, and if your customers are on social media, it's something that you should address in your customer service program. Here are eight reasons for building a social media customer service program:

People are doing it
> The fact that 62% of all consumers have used social media for customer service issues suggests that Twitter and Facebook are no longer fringe technologies for communication. Regardless of whether you have enabled the Zendesk Twitter integration, your customers will probably still be tweeting about your product, brand, or service. There's a lot of value in recognizing that those tweets exist and starting to do something about it.

Low barrier to entry
> Throughout this book, we've mentioned the relative ease of submitting tickets using the various channels. Email tends to be a customer favorite, because most people are already familiar with it. However, customers are increasingly becoming more comfortable communicating via Twitter and Facebook. In the very near future, these channels may surpass email as the preferred communication method for people who need to voice a concern with your company. The risk with social media is that when customers express themselves using this channel, other people can also read the conversation.

Opportunity for positive publicity
> Most of the time, you'll solve support requests quietly and privately. This is because the customer service process is typically private. When social media is thrown into the mix, the conversation becomes more public. You can take advantage of this fact

---

and demonstrate to your customers that you are speaking to your customers positively and supportively. As an example, If you take a look at @Ask_WellsFargo (*http://www.twitter.com/@Ask_WellsFargo*) on Twitter right now, we bet you'll see Wells Fargo Bank offering proactive assistance to its customers. This gives a very positive impression of the bank.

Social media is loud

This is the other edge of the social media sword. I mentioned in the previous item that Twitter gives you an opportunity for positive publicity, which is true, but it also gives you an opportunity for bad publicity. Unless you quickly defuse negative customer service situations with your customers, a simple tweet could very easily escalate into an embarrassing situation for your brand.

Proactively solve customer complaints

Not every customer who tweets to your organization expects a response. A great example of this occurred in 2011, with what has been described as "the greatest customer service story ever told." Peter Shankman (a well-known social media expert) was having a busy day and missed dinner at his favorite steakhouse before having to catch a flight, so he casually tweeted to Morton's Steakhouse to ask them to meet him with a steak when he landed a few hours later. At the time, Peter wasn't expecting a response. When he landed, he was greeted by a member of the Morton's Steakhouse waitstaff, who had brought him a steak. Obviously a member of the Morton's customer service team had seen Peter's tweet, and realized the potential to satisfy one of its customers. The amount of publicity that Morton's received from this event was huge, because Peter Shankman blogged about the incident on his website (*http://bit.ly/great-steak*). This is a great example that shows the opportunity created when customers tweet to your organization. I can't guarantee that Morton's is using Zendesk to provide customer service, but if you implement the Twitter integration in your Zendesk instance, you are certainly one step closer to this kind of experience.

Reactively respond to customer concerns

According to a study mentioned earlier, 58% of the people who tweet a complaint expect a response from that company. The sheer volume of this number—which is the majority of customers—reiterates the importance of having a social media presence on Twitter. A tweet that goes unnoticed could lead to customer dissatisfaction, and a quiet departure from the use of your product or service.

Announcements can be broadcast

As you start to build your social media customer service presence using Zendesk, you'll find that the number of followers on your Twitter handle also increases. A side benefit of having these additional followers is that when your company needs to make an important announcement, it becomes very easy to communicate with a large number of people. Nurturing and building the size of your community, whether you're on social media or not, is a key pillar in the process of providing outstanding customer service.

Distribution of ideas

If one of your customers tweets to you, "I can't log into your website" and you reply —via Zendesk—with the tweet, "We have a list of possible causes for this issue in our knowledge base," this has the obvious benefit that the recipient will get the message. It will also have a secondary benefit, which is that other people who are monitoring your Twitter channel will see the same message. These people may be customers or members of your community, or they may be your own team members. The information in your tweet may come to mind when another person needs the same information, and that person will know the answer to his question without submitting a support ticket. As your social media presence builds, people will start to subscribe to your channels just for these tips and tricks, which builds your community and increases your ability to broadcast important messages, as described in the previous point.

Ticket Sharing

In 2011, a few organizations got together and launched an initiative named Networked Help Desk (*http://www.networkedhelpdesk.org*). The goal of the project was to create a framework for better communication between various software tools, particularly the tools in the customer service space. Zendesk is one of the founding members of Networked Help Desk, and one of the first tangible benefits of the new framework was the "Ticket Sharing" feature released inside Zendesk. In a nutshell, this feature allows your organization to seamlessly, transparently, and automatically synchronize support tickets with other systems. This is considered a channel in Zendesk even though there is no administration settings page for it under Channels. The ticket sharing settings are found on the "Ticket Sharing" tab on the Tickets administration page.

A very common use case for this feature is when your organization is using Zendesk, and your partners, customers, and/or vendors are also using the tool. Using ticket sharing, there is no need to take customer service conversations out of Zendesk and into email when your organization is working with another company. This feature is offered on all Zendesk plans. It supports non-Zendesk applications (such as Atlassian JIRA) and custom applications as well, but in this book we will focus on Zendesk-to-Zendesk integrations.

To get started with this feature, you'll need to open the "Ticket sharing" tab on the Tickets administration page. There are two different types of agreements:

Sending agreement

This is when your organizations would like to send tickets to another Zendesk instance. For example, if you are a software company and you have a vendor that writes integrations for you, you might use this type of agreement to send tickets over to your vendor when a bug with an integration is reported. On the other side, the vendor will receive a new ticket with a message saying that it has been shared from your instance.

Receiving agreement

This is an agreement that says that you've authorized another Zendesk instance to share tickets with your Zendesk instance, meaning that another company can create tickets in your Zendesk instance via ticket sharing. For example, if you're the vendor writing a software integration and the other company is the provider, this type of agreement would allow the other company to share bug reports with you.

 Sending agreements are not automatically reciprocated. If you request to send tickets to another company and it accepts the invite, that will mean that you can send tickets to it, and that the contents of those tickets will be synchronized, but it does not automatically mean that the company can send new tickets back to you. If you'd like a reciprocated relationship, both parties are required to create a new sending agreement, originating from each Zendesk instance. Setting up a reciprocal arrangement is not necessary in all situations, though.

Ticket Sharing Example

Another good example of this feature is the ticket sharing agreement between the Zendesk Support instance and the Zen U instance. Because the support team and the training team are different departments at Zendesk, each has its own Zendesk instance. When the support team receives a new ticket saying, "I'd like to request a custom training time," it clicks the button to share with the Zen U instance and a new ticket is created there. As the training team answers the inquiry, the comments and status are updated over on the Zendesk Support instance automatically. Alternatively, when a ticket is received on the Zen U instance that says, "I can't log into Zendesk," this will be shared with the Zendesk Support team. When the support team answers the inquiry, the synchronization will automatically update the ticket on the Zen U instance, and the status will be set to solved when the ticket is complete.

From the ticket sharing tab, you'll need to click the "add sharing invite" link and select Zendesk. This is the process to create a sending agreement, which will allow your Zendesk instance to send tickets to another instance. There are four options on this page:

Partner Zendesk domain

This is the subdomain selected by the partner when it sets up its Zendesk instance. It'll need to tell you this domain so you can set it up on your side.

Comment and status permissions

The question to answer here is: do you want to allow your partner company to be able to make comments that are going to be visible to your customers, and to update the status of your tickets? This is an important decision, because there might be a situation where your partner company should not communicate with your customers directly. If this is the case, you would set this option to allow only private comments. The status field is linked to the comment visibility in this option because the use cases to update each of these fields are highly coupled. In other words, if your partner is given permission to publish public comments, it is effectively assigned ownership over the ticket, so it should also be able to solve the ticket. If you've restricted the partner to making only private comments, then it's logical that you would want to control the status of the ticket on your side. By default, all comments and statuses are shared in ticket sharing agreements.

Tag synchronization

Synchronization of tags means that any tags that are added to the ticket on the partner side will also be added to the ticket on your side, and vice versa. This would usually not be an problem, except that tags can also have an impact on custom fields. If a tag is shared and it matches a tag that you've assigned to one of the drop-down list options in your custom field, that option will automatically (and probably erroneously) be selected in your ticket. This can cause problems if you have a strict business process or business rules connected to the tags, so it might be safest to keep tag synchronization disabled in this situation. If your business process is less closely tied to tags, we recommend that you enable synchronization of tags, just to provide better communication of information between tickets. By default, tags are not shared in ticket sharing agreements.

Allow the syncing of custom fields

If you're working very closely with your partner and have a strong knowledge of its custom fields (or, even better, access to configure its Zendesk instance), you might use this feature. It adds a new level of synchronization to the tickets in both instances by automatically ensuring that all custom field values are kept the same. If the Zendesk instance of the other company is relatively unknown, though, it would be risky to enable this feature. This option is disabled by default on new ticket sharing agreements.

After you've selected your options, click the "Send invite" button. This will send an email to all administrators of the other Zendesk instance, asking them to confirm the sharing invitation. One of those administrators must confirm the invitation before tickets can be shared, but after it has been accepted, you can start sharing tickets immediately. Agents share tickets manually by selecting the Zendesk instance from the drop-down list beneath "Share ticket with" on the ticket summary screen.

After a ticket is shared, it's not possible for you to find the ticket ID of tickets on both sides of the sharing agreement, and the simple reason for this is privacy. Because it's impossible to know the relationship between your company and the other company with which you are sharing your tickets, Zendesk does not provide any information about the ticket on the other company's Zendesk instance, aside from the fact that the ticket is shared, and the standard ticket details such as fields and the names of the people who have added comments.

 If you're using the Enterprise plan, it's possible for you to automate the process of sharing tickets (see "Triggers" on page 132). This can be useful when you want to automatically send tickets to your partners and vendors. For example, on the Enterprise plan, you might add a trigger that finds all tickets with the phrase "integration bug" in the subject line, and automatically shares those tickets with the Zendesk instance of your software development vendor. It saves a manual triage process on behalf of the agent who would share the ticket with the vendor manually anyway.

CHAPTER 6

Fields and Data Capture

When your customers submit a support ticket, they'll use *fields* to describe their problem. For example, the Subject field describes the problem briefly, and the Description field provides further details that are used to solve the request. When the agent receives the ticket, he'll want to judge the severity, then forward it to the right people to solve it. This will involve use of the Priority, Group, and Assignee fields. Sometimes, the standard fields in Zendesk aren't sufficient to describe the issue succinctly, or there is a situation where a customer should be prompted to enter more specific details about her issue. If this is the case, *custom fields* can be used to capture new information. This section covers the various types of fields in Zendesk, including each of the fields mentioned here.

Data Capture Lifecycle

When customers open the ticket submission page on a default Zendesk instance, they will be prompted to enter a subject and description only. The screen that most end users see is shown in Figure 6-1.

As an administrator, you are able to add custom fields (covered on page 104) to the ticket submission page, which will prompt users to enter additional information about their requests. This process is often valuable because custom fields can remind the user about the information agents might find useful to solve a request. Figure 6-2 shows an example of a ticket submission form with custom fields included.

You'll notice that this screen has some optional fields and required fields. We review the recommended practices for using required fields on page 90.

After the ticket has been created and its ID has been assigned, the ticket will appear in the view of the agent assigned to it. The exact process for an agent to find a new ticket will vary. Some organizations like to proactively use the default "Unassigned tickets" to find tickets to be processed, whereas others prefer to wait for an email notification to appear in the agent's inbox before signing into Zendesk to start working on tickets. The choice between these options comes down mainly to the volume of tickets received by your organization. If your organization gets one new ticket per day, it would be a waste of time for your agents to stay signed into Zendesk all day. It's best to use effective email notifications (discussed more on page 147) in a situation where your volume is low.

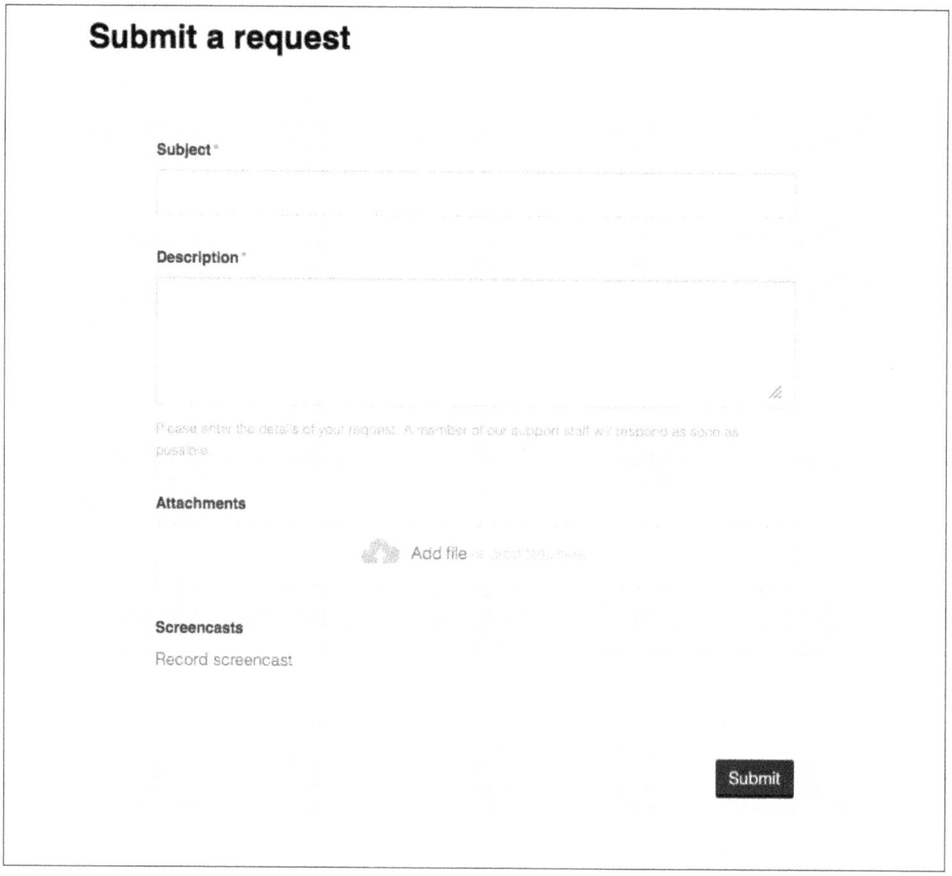

Submit a request

Subject *

Description *

Please enter the details of your request. A member of our support staff will respond as soon as possible.

Attachments

Add file

Screencasts

Record screencast

Submit

Figure 6-1. Default ticket submission form for end users

Ideally, the workflow for agents to find tickets and start working on them should be implemented on an organization-wide basis to create some consistency. In reality, every agent has a unique personality, so it's also a good practice to allow your agents to subtly vary their personal ticket workflow from the standard organizational workflow. Our advice is to set a standard workflow, educate agents on that workflow, and then allow your agents to make the decision on how they work most effectively. An example of the new ticket completed by the end user, but viewed from the agent's perspective, is demonstrated in Figure 6-3.

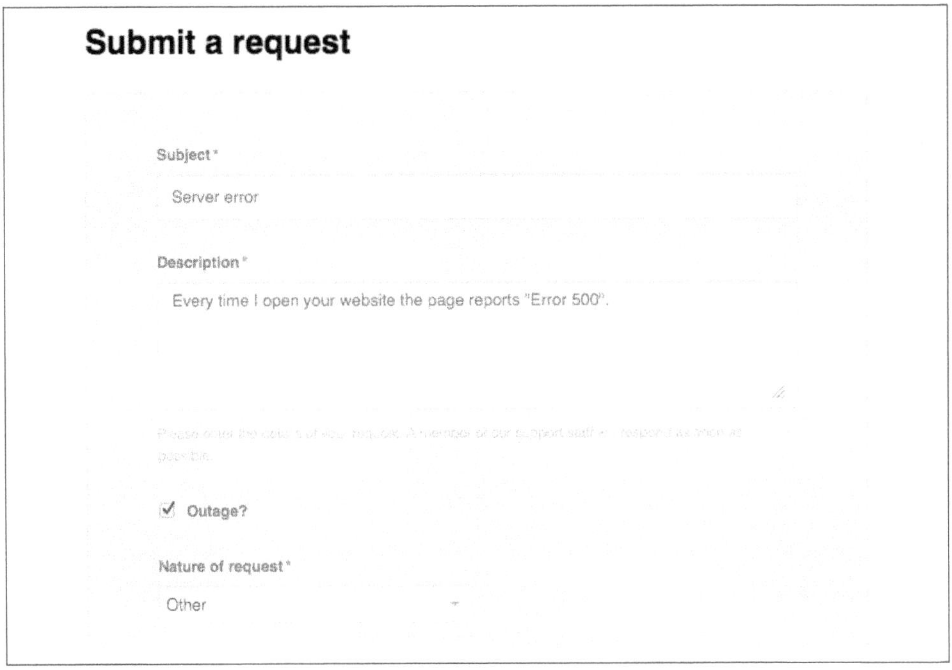

Figure 6-2. Ticket submission form including custom fields for end users

When an agent reads a ticket for the first time, he should be looking at the fields on that ticket for red flags. For example, the words *outage* or *urgent* would suggest that the agent needs to raise the priority of the ticket to get it to the right people very quickly. Regardless of the severity of the incident though, it's best for your agent to update all fields immediately. This process is also called *triaging* a ticket. Ideally, a properly triaged ticket should not appear in the view where the agent found it originally. After the ticket triage process is complete, it might look similar to Figure 6-4.

After all fields have been updated according to the agent's perception of the issue, the agent should submit the ticket to save the updated fields. If the agent did not have the opportunity to complete the triage process, he should submit the ticket in the New status, which flags the ticket for triage by another member of the team. Otherwise, if the agent has already triaged the ticket, he should submit the ticket in the Open status. If the agent assigned the ticket to himself, he might start working on the ticket. Otherwise, the agent to which it's assigned might get an email notification or sign into Zendesk directly to find tickets assigned to her for action. The new agent will read all the fields completed by the first agent, and start working on the ticket immediately.

Figure 6-3. Fields on a new ticket from the agent's perspective

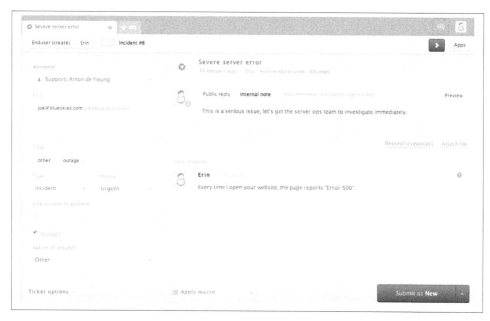

Figure 6-4. Fields on a ticket after being updated by an agent

End-User Fields

If you open the "Ticket fields" administration page and click the "edit" link for any of the system or custom fields, you'll see a page similar to Figure 6-5. This page allows you to configure the options for the field.

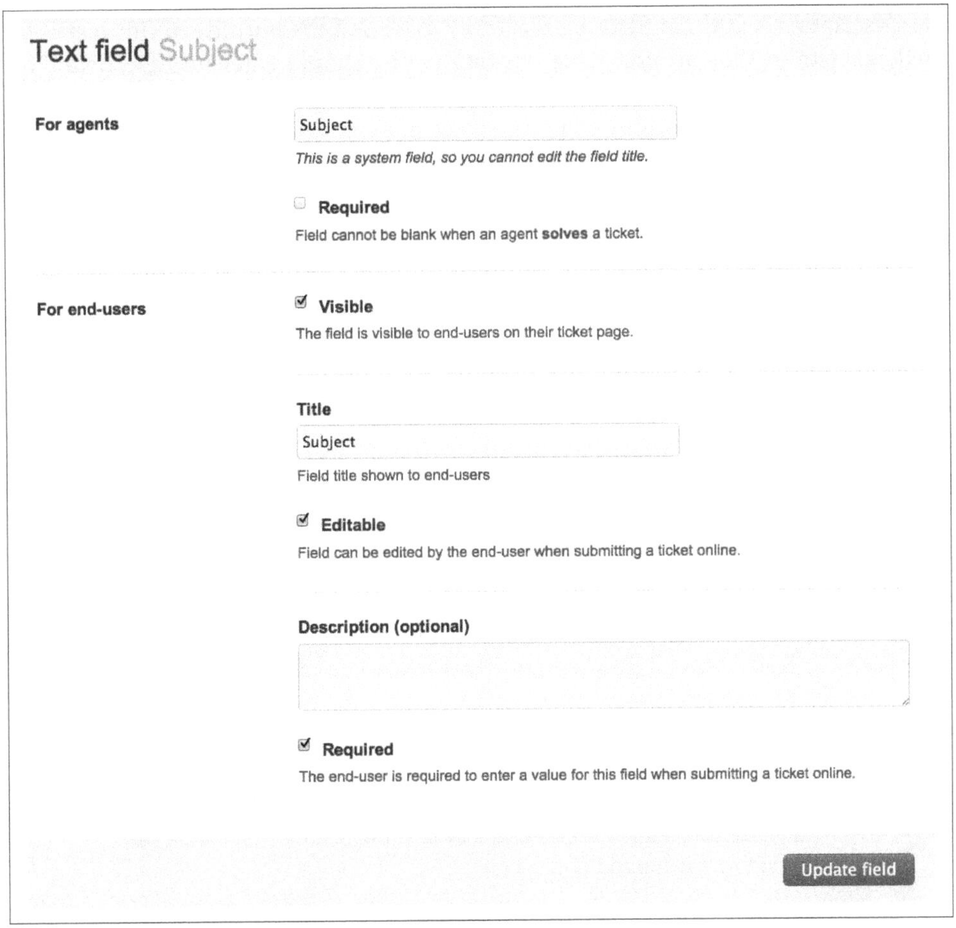

Figure 6-5. Administration page for the Subject system field

When you select the Visible checkbox beside the "For end users" option on the Field administration page, a new section will be expanded, with an option that allows you to change the Title of the field for end users. This Title will be visible on the end-user interface only, and is separate from the field Title that is set for agents and administrators at the very top of this page.

The option to make a field visible to an end user is granted to administrators only, and it's not possible for an agent to select which individual fields will be visible to the end user. If you've configured a field to be visible or editable by end users, the field will always be visible, regardless of the type or status of a ticket.

The Description text is configurable for every field, and the purpose of this text is to briefly explain to the end user what information he should enter into the field. For example, if a field prompted the user to indicate the severity of his issue, the description text for that field might include some examples of other issues with the same level of severity. The description text is visible only to end users on the ticket submission form, and is not visible to agents or administrators on the ticket page or submission form.

The other option on the field administration page is a checkbox to make the field editable by end users. By default, most of the ticket fields are not editable by end users, and there is a very good reason for this. If end users can change fields, you lose some control over your business process and reporting. As an example, if you're capturing metrics on the number of incidents reported versus the number of questions and your customers have permission to edit this field, they might not select the correct field in every situation and your metrics will not be accurate. Agents are trained on which fields to select, based on specific criteria for your organization.

On the other hand, making fields editable by end users may help a lot with the triage process. It is possible, using triggers as described in "Triggers" on page 132, to configure an automatic business rule that checks the values entered by the end user when she creates a ticket, then assigns the ticket to a specific team based on those values. The other scenario is that you might want your customers to provide as much information as possible during the ticket creation to make it easier for your agents to diagnose the support request.

It's not possible in Zendesk for a field to contain one value for agents and another value for end users, even if the name of the field is different for agents and end users.

Required Fields

In the previous section, we explained the value of asking for detailed information from customers, the end result of which is that the agent will be able to solve the support request more effectively. However, a common mistake by administrators is to make too many fields required. The problem with an extensive set of required fields is that it forces the customer to put a lot of effort into the process of submitting a support request, which is an unpleasant customer service experience from the very start. Customers may grow frustrated and decline to complete the process, and may stop using your service altogether because they don't feel like it's easy to work with your organization. This idea is also contrary to Zendesk's "low barrier to entry" philosophy, which is to make it as simple and easy as possible for everyone to achieve tasks in the product.

If it's necessary to make a field required, because the support ticket would not be complete without it, you can do this via the Field administration page. Zendesk views fields as "required" in two different ways:

Required for end users

This is the most conventional type of required field, where the ticket submission form cannot be submitted without a value being entered in the text box. An asterisk appears next to the name of the field to indicate that the field is required. To make a field required for end users, select the Required checkbox beside the "For end users" option on the Field administration page.

Required for agents

To make it as easy as possible for agents to do their jobs, in Zendesk you cannot force an agent to complete any field except the Description field during the ticket creation process. Even if the field is marked as required for agents, it does not need a value when the ticket is created. The concept of a field being required for agents applies only to solving the request. In other words, if the Type field is required for agents, a ticket can be created without a value for Type, but when the agent solves the request, that agent must enter a value for this field. To make a field required for agents, select the Required checkbox beside the "For agents" option on the Field administration page.

The Description field is required for all agents and all end users, so none of these options are editable on the Description field.

 In special circumstances in the product, it is possible for a required field to not contain a value. Some examples are when the custom field was added to Zendesk after a ticket was already solved, or if the ticket was solved during the process of solving a problem. For this reason, you should not rely heavily on a field always having a value when performing business processes.

System Fields

Out of the box, a standard Zendesk instance starts with a number of *system fields*, each with a specific purpose. An administrator can configure most of these system fields in the Ticket fields administration page, and some other fields can be configured through various administrative sections of the product.

This section takes a high-level approach to your use of fields in Zendesk. The next section will explain each of the individual system fields in more detail and focus on the specific options for that field.

 In general, most of Zendesk's system fields are worth enabling and should be used for their intended purpose. For one thing, parts of Zendesk make assumptions about how you are using them. We occasionally see customers use the system fields for nonconventional purposes, but it rarely works successfully.

Your ideal process would be to educate your agents on the meaning and interpretation of each of the system fields, based on the following summary:

ID
> Numeric field that uniquely identifies every ticket.

Subject
> Brief explanation of the support request, without going into specific details.

Description
> More detailed description of the issue experienced by the customer, which should be enough information to solve the ticket.

Requester
> The person who needs assistance.

CC
> The other people who are interested in receiving email notifications when the ticket is updated.

Status
> Stage in the lifecycle of a ticket, whether it has not yet been triaged (New), is currently being answered (Open), is waiting for customer feedback (Pending), is answered (Solved), or is completed and locked for further updates (Closed).

Type
> The nature of the support request, whether it's a request for information (Question), a request to make a change or a request between customer service team members (Task), an occurrence of something that is not working (Incident), or a systemic issue that is causing many related Incidents to occur (Problem).

Priority
> Level of urgency that should be applied to the ticket, based on a small list of options. Helps to determine which tickets should be answered first or need the most attention.

Group
> The team members at your organization who are assigned to work on this ticket.

Assignee
> Individual person at your organization working on the ticket, who will belong to the group selected on the ticket.

Tags
> Individual words that can be used to categorize a ticket, or to improve our ability to search for the ticket in Zendesk. Visible to agents and administrators but not visible to end users.

Comments
> A textual conversation between the viewers of a ticket—requester, assignee, and other agents—that will assist the process of solving the support request.

Attachments
> Files that can be included on the ticket when a comment is being added.

An Optional Status: On-Hold

In all of the Zendesk plans except the Starter plan, you can add an extra status called On-hold. It's not included as one of the default statuses, so you'll have to enable it in the Ticket fields administration page before using it. The purpose of this status, and the reason you might want to enable it, is to track tickets that need input from a third party —in other words, tickets that your agents can't solve. This can be an important distinction to make if you track your agents' performance. By filtering out tickets set to On-hold, you can get a more accurate picture of how your agents are actually performing because you've excluded the tickets that need information from a third party.

To the ticket requester, an On-hold ticket is simply an open ticket—the requestor is not aware that the agent is seeking information from some other, usually external, source.

System Field Configuration

The degree to which you can customize the Zendesk system fields is limited, because these fields play a big part in how Zendesk fundamentally functions. Some of the fields, such as Priority, have a bit more flexibility, and organizations occasionally elect not to use this field in their Zendesk implementation. The following section explains the options for all of the system fields, and the decision processes for implementation of them.

Ticket ID

Every ticket in your Zendesk instance will have a *ticket ID*, which is a unique and incrementing number assigned to the ticket when it is created. The format of the ticket

ID cannot be customized to include any characters other than this number. The only control that an administrator has over the ticket ID field is the number at which it should start. In the Tickets administration page, the Ticket IDs option can be increased to any number you like. Some customers elect to set the number higher than 2 (which is the default on a new Zendesk instance), to ensure that more digits are used in ticket IDs from the very start.

Ticket IDs are never recycled, which means that if you create ticket number 17 and ticket number 18, then delete ticket number 17, the next ticket will still be ticket number 19. Ticket number 17 no longer exists in your Zendesk instance, and will never exist again.

Subject

The value in the *Subject* field of a ticket should be brief, and it will be truncated if someone enters more than 150 characters. That is, any characters beyond the 150th character will be removed from the subject entirely. This field is used in the subject line of email notifications and search results, which is another reason for it to be brief. Specific details about the issue should not be described in the Subject field, because this is the purpose of the Description field. The Subject field in the support ticket is very similar in concept to the subject line in an email.

From an administrator's perspective, it's interesting to note that, by default, the Subject field is not required for agents, either when creating a ticket or solving it. It's also possible to deactivate this field, though we strongly recommend against doing this. When a ticket is created without a value in the Subject field, Zendesk will use the first few words from the description in place of the subject line in some situations, or it will refer to the ticket by its ID.

Just to keep things consistent, we recommend that all administrators make the Subject field required for agents and end users. This still won't guarantee that your agents will enter a subject during the ticket submission process (because, as described earlier, that's not possible), but it will ensure that they enter a value during the solving process, and when you check a historical list of solved tickets, all of those tickets will have a subject included.

Description

The purpose of the *Description* field is to capture the details of the support request, which help the agent to solve it. In many ways, the Description field is simply the first comment on the ticket, and after the ticket is created, the description appears as the first comment and will scroll away from the top of the page like all of the other comments. A description is special, however, in that it cannot be made private, and the end user will always be able to read the Description field. The text entered in the Description field will be truncated and removed after 64,000 characters.

As mentioned previously, the Description field is required for all users, so the options to configure this field on the field administration page are limited.

Sometimes organizations use a standard phone line (i.e., not Zendesk Voice) to provide support to customers, and they find it frustrating that the description of a ticket, which is also the first comment, must be visible to the customer. The problem, from their perspective, is that the agent is on the phone with the customer and would like to enter private information into the ticket, but cannot easily do so. One possible solution for this problem is to instruct the agent to enter the text "Customer phone call" in the Description field and create the ticket immediately, then enter more private information as a subsequent comment and mark that comment as an internal note. The result is that the end user will see a generic description, but not the private internal notes in the Comment field.

Carbon Copy (CC)

The *CC* field is one that is very useful, but disabled by default. We encourage all administrators to immediately enable the CC field in their Zendesk instance by opening the Tickets administration page and selecting the "Enable CCs on tickets" checkbox. The concept is very similar to the CC field in email: anyone CC'ed on a ticket will automatically receive an email update when a new comment is added to the ticket. The similarities are not exact, but it's a relevant analogy.

The CC field is also a way of allowing end users other than the requester to view a ticket in the Help Center. If a ticket is relevant to multiple people and there are no privacy or security concerns, it's possible to add multiple end-user accounts (up to 24) to the list of CC'ed users, and those end users will all be able to view the ticket when visiting the Zendesk Help Center. It's possible to add an unlimited number of agent accounts as CC'ed users on a ticket.

After enabling the CC feature on the Tickets administration page, you will see some other options on this page that can be configured. One of the options is labeled "Only agents can add CCs." This option helps to ensure that your customers do not give access to tickets to other people unknowingly, by restricting the privilege of CC'ing another user to agents only.

 When an end user wants to CC other end users, he can do this only by CCing that person on an email sent to your Zendesk instance. The Zendesk Help Center does not currently allow end users to CC other people from their web browsers.

Requester

From an administrator's perspective, there are very few options to be configured for the *Requester* field. This field identifies the profile of the person who needs assistance. Sometimes an agent will submit a ticket on behalf of the customer, in which case the customer is the requester, and the agent is the *submitter*. This relationship is indicated using the word "via." For example, "Erin EndUser via Stafford Vaughan" indicates that Stafford submitted the ticket on behalf of Erin, either through the Help Center or one of the other channels. It's also possible for an agent to create the requester's user profile at the same time as she creates the ticket.

Ticket Status

The five *Status* fields are built into the product and cannot be changed or extended by an administrator. The general principle behind this decision is that "less is more," and as the author of the *Atlassian JIRA Workflows* training course, Stafford can tell you that whenever a workflow is customizable, the complexity of the software rises significantly.

The statuses can be summarized as follows:

New

> The ticket has not yet been evaluated or assigned to be answered by a support agent, and there is a good chance—though not a guarantee—that the ticket was created recently. Tickets in this status are some of the most important, because the nature of the request is generally unknown, and could be as severe as an outage that needs immediate attention. All tickets created by end users in Zendesk will be placed into the New status, but after they move out of the new status, it's no longer possible to put them back into this status.

Open

> The ticket and its fields have been evaluated by a support agent, and someone is probably working on the ticket. If a ticket in the New status is assigned to an agent, its status will automatically be changed to Open. A ticket could also be in the Open status without an assignee, which means that it still needs to be assigned to someone for completion.

Pending

> The support agent assigned to this ticket cannot solve the ticket without additional information from the customer, and is waiting for the customer to provide that information. This status should not be used when the agent is waiting for more information from another agent or another department at the organization. This status should be used only when you're waiting for more information from the requester. Any emails or comments added by an end user to a ticket in this status will automatically move the ticket back into the open status.

On-hold

This optional status is similar to the Pending status in that the agent assigned to the ticket cannot solve it until he receives additional information. In this case, the information needed comes from a third party. To the requester, the On-hold status is shown as open. As mentioned earlier in this chapter, you won't see this status in your Zendesk instance unless you enable it.

Solved

Either the end user or the agent believes that the issue described in the support request no longer exists, or the work has been completed. While the ticket is in the Solved status, it can be moved back into the Open or Pending statuses. Any emails or comments added to the ticket by an end user while it is in this status will also automatically move the ticket back into the Open status, unless the end user is on the Help Center and has clicked the checkbox labeled "Please consider this request resolved."

Closed

The inquiry has been answered, a sufficient amount of time (the default is four days) has passed, and there is no more work to be done for the support request. When a ticket is moved into the Closed status, it is not possible to edit the ticket in any way. It's not possible to change the assignee, update tags, add comments, or move it back into any of the other statuses. The only task that can be performed on a closed ticket is to create a *follow-up* ticket, which is a completely new ticket with a link back to an existing closed ticket for reference. Any incoming emails related to a closed ticket will also create a follow-up ticket. It's important to note that users cannot manually move a ticket into the Closed status, and the only way to close a ticket is by using a trigger or automation. The only exception to this rule is when an agent merges tickets, which will have the side effect that the source ticket will be closed.

Typically, the workflow of a ticket will follow the order in which the statuses appear in this list.

The Status field is not visible to end users, so it's also not possible to make it editable by end users. Instead of seeing these statuses, end users see a brief sentence instead. Here is the list of sentences provided to end users:

New

This request is awaiting assignment to a help desk operator.

Open

This request is currently being processed by our staff.

Pending

This request is awaiting your response.

Solved/Closed
> This request has been deemed solved.

When you are configuring the Status field, you may notice that the Visible checkbox is disabled, suggesting that it's not visible to the end users. This is not quite true, it's just that you can't control the visibility.

 One of the most common mistakes customers make with Zendesk is using the Pending status in the wrong way. Zendesk has some default automations that will send email reminders to the requester of the ticket after 24 hours and again after 5 days of the ticket being in the Pending state. These automations are described in "Default Automations" on page 141. If you use the Pending status while the ticket is waiting for further information from someone else on the support team, the customer will be very confused when he starts receiving emails asking him to respond to the request. For this reason, it's important that your agents always limit their use of the Pending status to when they are waiting for further information from the customer.

Ticket Types

As with the status, Zendesk has a standard set of options for the *Type* field, which are not configurable by the administrator. Because the Type field is one that can be deactivated, I've seen situations in which some administrators decided that this field would not be used at all in their Zendesk instance. After reading this section and understanding the Type field, you should decide whether it's relevant for your usage of the product.

There are four possible options for the Type field, which can be summarized as follows:

Question
> We generally reserve this type for tickets where the steps required to answer the support request do not require any changes to be made by the agent or the support team. This interpretation will allow you to produce reports on the volume of questions in your Zendesk instance, then proactively record the answers to those questions in the Help Center (see Chapter 9).

Incident
> An Incident is something that has gone wrong, and needs to be fixed. An example of an Incident is when a customer submits a ticket saying, "I cannot sign into your website." From the customer's perspective, she understands the symptoms of the issue and will describe those symptoms in the ticket. The Incident is usually the description of the symptoms.

Problem

> When a customer submits the Incident just described, an agent will start to investigate the issue. She might discover that the customer cannot sign in to the website because the authentication server is down. This is known as the "root cause" of the Incident, and it is considered to be the *Problem*. A Problem will typically be the root cause of many similar Incidents.

Task

> Tasks will represent a request for a change, or an internal activity carried out by agents. An easy way to think about the difference between a Task and an Incident is that if an Incident is reported, something has gone wrong. Often, nothing has gone wrong when a Task is submitted. Maybe some sort of activity just needs to take place, or a change is necessary. This is very commonly used in IT or internal customer service centers. The Task type also features a Due Date field that allows agents to indicate when the Task is due for completion, and business rules can be connected to this date to provide reminders if necessary.

Zendesk has a useful feature that allows agents to link several Incidents to the same Problem. When the Problem is solved, all of the connected Incidents will automatically be solved at the same time. This feature saves a great deal of time for agents, and ensures that the message provided during the resolution of the Problem will consistently be distributed to all of the end users who are experiencing the same issue. Most people consider this to be the primary benefit of using the Type field in Zendesk (although we personally like the idea of tracking questions and turning them into knowledge base articles).

The general rule is that only agents should create Problems in Zendesk, though some companies don't follow this rule. We recommend this practice because if a customer submits a ticket that is marked as a Problem and it is the primary ticket on which agents add comments, there is a strong possibility that one of those agents will make the mistake of publishing a sensitive comment and not marking it as private. This situation is far more likely to occur on a Problem, which will be actively used by agents to solve the root cause, versus the Incident, which is just a specific example of the impact of the issue. To avoid the risk of end users being sent information that is potentially sensitive, the Problem ticket should always be created by an agent, and end users should never see it.

It's possible for administrators to make the Type field visible and editable by end users, though we don't recommend it because there is a strong likelihood that end users will mark requests as the wrong type, and the metrics described earlier will not be accurate.

Priority

The options allowed in the *Priority* field are Low, Medium, High, and Urgent. If you prefer to use only two priorities, you can change these options on the Priority field administration page to include just Normal and High. It's not possible to create a custom set of priorities, though it is possible to deactivate the Priority field altogether, and add "Custom Fields" on page 104 to include a custom set of priorities selected by your organization.

By default, the Priority field is visible to end users, but not editable. Administrators often make the mistake of thinking that since the Priority field is not visible when end users create a ticket, they will not see the Priority field after the agent triages the ticket. This causes negative feelings with customers when the agent selects Low priority for her ticket, and the end user sees this classification on the ticket summary page. To prevent this issue, you should immediately set the Priority field to be not visible to end users. The reality is that customers will often misinterpret your perception of the various priorities anyway, so it doesn't add a lot of value for them to be able to see the Priority that the agent has selected.

If you would like to set up Zendesk to have separate "internal priority" and "customer priority" fields, it's possible to do this by adding a new custom field. I've seen companies use this approach successfully, and it's a good way for customers to feel like their voice is heard, without dictating the actions of your support agents. If you take this approach, it's very important that you ensure that the internal priority field is not visible to end users. If a customer selects High in the customer Priority field and the agent has selected Low in the internal Priority field, that disconnect could make your customer very angry.

Group and Assignee

The reason we've included both the *Group* and *Assignee* fields together in this section is that, when it comes to the ticket page, they are tightly connected. The purpose of the Group field on the ticket page is to funnel the ticket into the relevant set of agents. For example, if an agent was escalating a ticket, he might select Level 2 Support as the group. The result of this change would be that the list of agents in the Assignee field would include only the agents who are in the Level 2 Support group. This makes it easier for the agent to ensure that the ticket goes to the most suitable agent or agents to solve the request.

As an alternative to selecting the Group *and* Assignee, it's a valid practice to select just the Group. For example, if your company had several people responsible for the billing process but the agent wasn't sure which specific person should handle an inquiry, he can change the group to Billing (after it had been created by an administrator), then leave the Assignee field blank. The default triggers in Zendesk will automatically send an email to all members of the Billing group with a message that a ticket has been assigned to the entire group. The same technique could be used for the Level 2 Support group just described, or any other group in the system. In fact, this is probably more common and a better practice than assigning tickets to a specific member of the group, just because it provides more flexibility on which members of the support team will address a specific inquiry.

It's possible for an administrator to make the Group and Assignee fields visible to end users, but it is not possible for you to make either field editable by end users. The reason why end users should not select the group is that you'll end up with a situation where end users always select the Level 2 Support or Managers group, and the reason that end users should not select an Assignee is that only the support agents know whether or not that agent is able to handle the specific request. Customers should not be able to dictate which members of your support team will handle their inquiry.

 The Assignee field lists only the agents in your Zendesk instance, and will never include end users. Even though an end user may be the person whose responsibility it is to provide the next response, this situation can be expressed by an appropriately set Pending status, which implicitly suggests that the ticket requester is now working on the ticket.

Tags

You should think of *tags* as the "glue" that holds all business rules in Zendesk together. Tags are used extensively in business rules, as described in "Triggers" on page 132 and "Automations" on page 140. Tags also allow administrators to provide more detailed reports to their support managers, and at a very basic level, they help agents search for tickets. The contents of the Tags field are visible to administrators and agents, but are never visible to end users.

The Tags field is not listed on the Ticket fields administration page, because it isn't configured in the same way as many of the other system fields. Administrators can enable and disable this field using the "Enable tags on tickets" checkbox on the Tickets administration page. If you are on the Enterprise plan, it's also possible to grant or deny agents the ability to tag tickets at the agent-role level, giving only some agents the permission to use tags, and hiding the Tags field from other agents.

If you have enabled tags in your instance, you'll notice another option labeled "Enable automatic ticket tagging" on the Tickets administration page. This is enabled by default, but there are certain situations in which I strongly discourage administrators from enabling this option. This feature will check all new tickets created by end users, match those tickets against existing tickets, and tag the new ticket with exactly three tags, based on the set of tags added to similar tickets. This is usually a good thing because it makes searching and categorizing of tickets easier, but it can also cause problems if your business processes and rules are closely tied to the use of tags. A simple example is if an agent tags a ticket with "vip_customer" according to a specific business process, and then the automatic tagging function added this tag to a random ticket because it had properties similar to the first ticket—this would be a problem. The outcome of this situation is that the new ticket would be identified erroneously as being from a VIP customer, and the business process would break.

As an administrator, you will have access to the list of 100 most frequently used tags in the past two months on your Zendesk instance. The tags are presented in a *tag cloud*, which is a list of tags ordered by the frequency of use. An administrator can open this tag cloud from the Tags administration page, and remove a specific tag from all tickets —except those that are closed—by clicking on the tag, then selecting the appropriate link to delete all tags. A typical use for this feature would be if you find a meaningless tag such as "the" used frequently in your instance. The Tags administration page also allows you to see all tickets that are tagged with a specific tag, though it's possible to use search syntax to achieve the same purpose.

Comments

Comments are the "pulse" of a ticket. They help to keep a ticket active, maintain momentum during the support process, and are vital to an agent's ability to solve a ticket.

Comments typically contain information relevant to the support request (though I've seen some humorous examples where they are not related at all). Comments can be added by the agent solving the request, or by the customer who submitted the request. They can be questions, answers, or just private notes for your support team. Like the Tags field, the Comments field is not configured via the "Ticket fields" administration page. The settings for the Comments field are listed on the Tickets administration page.

The other settings on the Tickets administration page control the default visibility of the Comment field when agents add comments via the Help Center or email. By default, all new comments will be public and visible to the end users that have access to the ticket. If you'd prefer to make all new comments private—and plenty of companies select this option—it's possible to do this by deselecting the checkboxes on this page.

 You should start by making all new comments public, then either adjust these settings if you find that your agents are making mistakes with public comments, or work with your agents to ensure that they understand that comments not specifically marked as private will be visible to end users.

Markdown and Emoji

The default format for ticket comments is text; however, you can enable both Markdown and Emoji to allow your agents to add some basic formatting and a little humor to their comments. Both are optional settings on the Tickets administration page.

Markdown is a text-based markup language that provides simple formatting such as bold, italic, bullet lists, headings, and so on. Markdown is supported by many web technologies, which translate it to equivalent HTML; if your agents are tech-savvy, they may already know it and will appreciate being able to use it in Zendesk. If they don't already know it, it's simple and easy to learn.

Emoji, which is similar to emoticons and originated in Japan, is a collection of ideograms that represent a range of emotions (think of a smiley face), gestures, symbols, and pictures that can be inserted anywhere within a comment. These may not be appropriate for the more buttoned-down support organization, but they can add some fun and personalization to the conversation between the agent and end user.

Attachments

Just like when you add attachments to an email, Zendesk allows end users and agents to include *attachments* on a ticket. Attachments in Zendesk are typically files that assist the process of solving the support request, and augment the information in comments. Attachments are always added to comments (i.e., they cannot be added independently) and will be displayed in the context of the comment, which may require scrolling down the ticket page to find a specific attachment.

There is no limit on the type of files that can be attached to tickets, but the maximum size of each attachment is determined by the plan of your Zendesk instance. Starter plan customers can include attachments up to 1 MB each, Regular plan customers can include attachments up to 7 MB each, and Plus and Enterprise customers can attach files up to 20 MB each.

Administrators can configure the attachment settings on the Tickets administration page. The first option, "Customers can attach files," is intuitive and determines whether end users are able to attach files to the ticket. The other option on this page, "Private attachments," is a slightly bigger decision. The private attachments option will determine the level of security that is added to the attachments in your Zendesk instance. Because attachments are not attached to email notifications sent from Zendesk, the recipient of the email must click a link if he'd like to open the attachment. This link contains a randomized URL generated by Zendesk, and this randomization process provides a level of security. The option to make attachments directly accessible via the email link is the default setting in Zendesk, and is the easiest option for users because they just have to click a single link to access the attachment.

On the other hand, if you have serious concerns about security and would like an added layer of protection, you can require users to sign in with a username and password before they can access attachments, even if they used the randomly generated URL for the attachment. To enable this option, select the "Private attachments" checkbox on the Tickets administration page.

Screencasts

Zendesk has partnered with a company named Screenr to allow users to record screen capture videos inside Zendesk. The feature is known as *screencasting* and is available to organizations on the Plus and Enterprise plans. Screencasting is totally free, and both your agents and end users can use it to add videos to tickets.

Screencasting is useful for customers because sometimes, in order to explain their issue, they will need to write a long list of detailed steps to reproduce it—a process that can be rather frustrating. With the screencasts feature enabled, customers will have a link labeled "Record screencast" when submitting a ticket, which allows them to record their actions as a video instead of explaining their actions in words. It works just like the attachments feature, except there are a few more prompts for the user. When the process of recording the video is complete, the user can preview it, and then the video is added to the ticket for the agent to view. The customer will have the option of whether to include audio or not (for the less vocally inclined).

I should also note that it's possible for agents to record screencasts on tickets in the same way as end users. This can be useful if it's the agent who is trying to articulate a long list of steps, and would prefer to do that in video form.

In order for customers to use this feature, they will need to have the Java Runtime Environment installed on their computer. This is usually not an issue, because Java is installed on most modern computers by default.

Screencasts are disabled by default, and there are a few steps to enable this feature. If you visit the Tickets administration page, you'll notice the Screencasts option. If you select the "Enable screencasts for tickets" checkbox, you'll be immediately prompted to confirm that you'd like to link your Zendesk instance with Screenr. When you confirm this request, Zendesk creates a Screenr account for you in the background without requiring any further information from you. Once this process is complete, you'll receive a confirmation message, and the screencast feature will be enabled. Be sure to save the tab after the checkbox is checked. Once the feature is enabled, customers can immediately start recording screencasts on their tickets.

Custom Fields

There are two common use cases for *custom fields*, which are described in the following list. To add a custom field, go to the "Ticket fields" administration page and click "add custom field" in the upper-right corner. The list of fields will be presented along with examples of each (see Figure 6-6).

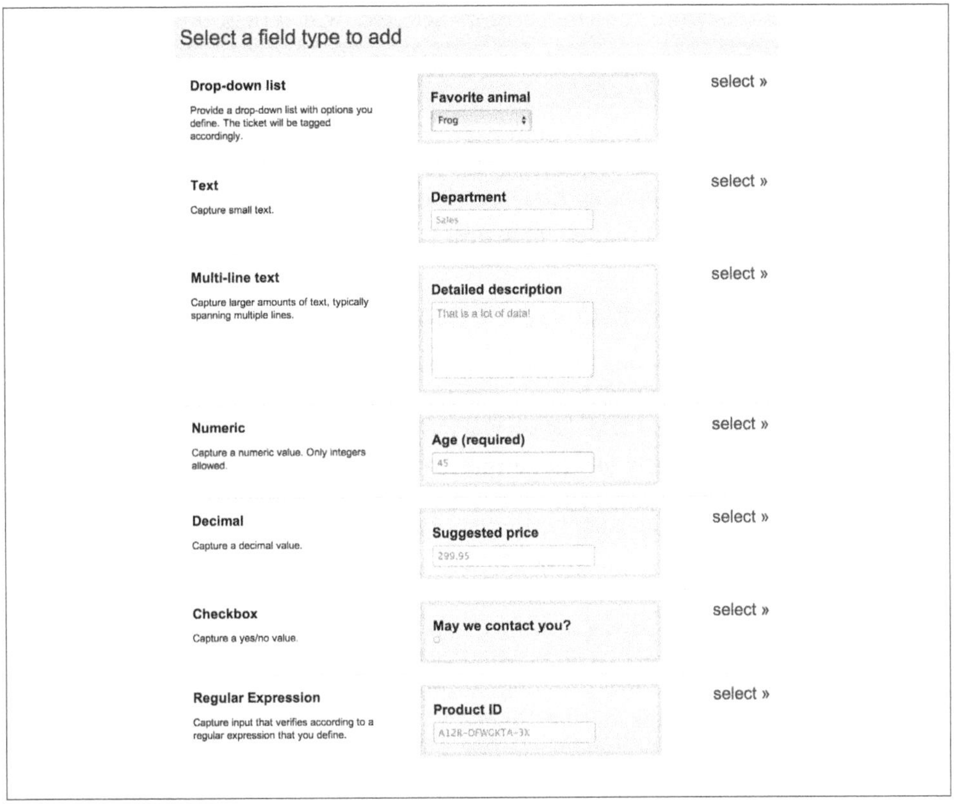

Select a field type to add

Drop-down list Provide a drop-down list with options you define. The ticket will be tagged accordingly.	**Favorite animal** Frog	select »
Text Capture small text.	**Department** Sales	select »
Multi-line text Capture larger amounts of text, typically spanning multiple lines.	**Detailed description** That is a lot of data!	select »
Numeric Capture a numeric value. Only integers allowed.	**Age (required)** 45	select »
Decimal Capture a decimal value.	**Suggested price** 299.95	select »
Checkbox Capture a yes/no value.	**May we contact you?**	select »
Regular Expression Capture input that verifies according to a regular expression that you define.	**Product ID** A12R-DFWGKTA-3X	select »

Figure 6-6. List of custom field options, along with examples of each

Agents requesting specific information from customers

At some stage in the life of every customer service team, it's likely that administrators or the support team will identify a piece of information so important to the process of answering support requests that it's worth asking every customer the same question. An example would be an "Outage occurring?" checkbox that allows the requester of the ticket to indicate whether her system is currently nonfunctional. This custom field would then feed into your support process, which may notify certain users of the outage.

Agents categorizing a ticket

The second use case for custom fields is when agents and administrators need to categorize tickets for reporting or execute a certain business process based on the agent's selection in a custom field. For example, you may add an About custom field, which has Database, User Interface, or User Management options. When agents triage tickets, they select one of these options. Administrators may define a process that would automatically send an email notification to certain people based on the selection in this field. Afterward, you may also like to run a report to identify the number of tickets with a certain category selected, which helps make predictions or identify trends.

Custom fields are useful because they collect all of the important pieces of information about a ticket at the top of the ticket summary screen, which makes it easier for agents to quickly find relevant pieces of information. The alternative to using custom fields is to hope that the end user provides the specific information in the comments, but even if she does, it can be difficult for an agent to find that information if it's scattered through the comment history.

The custom field options can be summarized as follows:

Drop-down list
> Also known as a "select list" in some circles, this field allows an administrator to specify the valid options from which the user may choose. It's a way of restricting the user response, usually for the purpose of categorizing the ticket. This type of field can be very useful when you're defining business rules, which might mandate that some action (such as "assign to a group" or "send an email notification") should occur based on a specific choice made by the user in this custom field.

Text and Multi-line text
> These options simply ask the user to enter a text value in an input box. The difference between the two is that the *Text* field appears on a single line only, whereas the *Multi-line text* field spans multiple lines.

Numeric and Decimal
> Both of these field types will present a text box to the user, but validate that the user has entered a number before allowing the user to submit the ticket form. The difference between these two fields is that the *Decimal* field supports the use of decimal points in the number, and the *Numeric* field requires the user to enter a whole number.

Checkbox
> This is our favorite type of custom field because it's very simple but also very powerful. When you start to define the tags that will be used by your triggers and automations in Zendesk, you'll appreciate the importance of getting those tags exactly right. Misspellings or misplaced dashes could be the difference between a successful or failed business process. The *Checkbox* custom field concept is simple: the administrator can define a tag that is associated with the checked state of the checkbox. When a user checks the box, that tag is added to the ticket. Simple. Less risk for your business processes, as well.

Regular Expression
> The last type of custom field is definitely the most complex, and probably the least frequently used. This type of field supports a *Regular Expression*, which is basically a special pattern that defines the valid format of the input from the user. Examples

of this feature would be a social security number, a phone number, or the serial number of your product. To define a regular expression custom field, the administrator must also define what the regular expression pattern must be, and the result is that any time a user enters a value in the field, her entry must match the correct format before the ticket can be submitted.

After you've selected the type of custom field, you'll be taken to the same field administration page as all of the system fields, except that the options will vary depending on the exact type of field that you've selected. When you've selected the options for your new custom field, click "Add field"; the field will be added to your Zendesk instance immediately.

Cascading Menus in Drop-Down Lists

If your drop-down list has a very large number of options and you would like those options to be categorized into cascading menus, you can use a special syntax in Zendesk to do this. When you define your field options for the "Drop-down list" field, you should use :: to indicate that a menu should be inserted. The :: needs to appear only in the Title of the option, and should not appear in the Tags for the option. An example of how to use this syntax is shown in Figure 6-7, which creates a menu labeled Software in the drop-down list, with three items inside that menu.

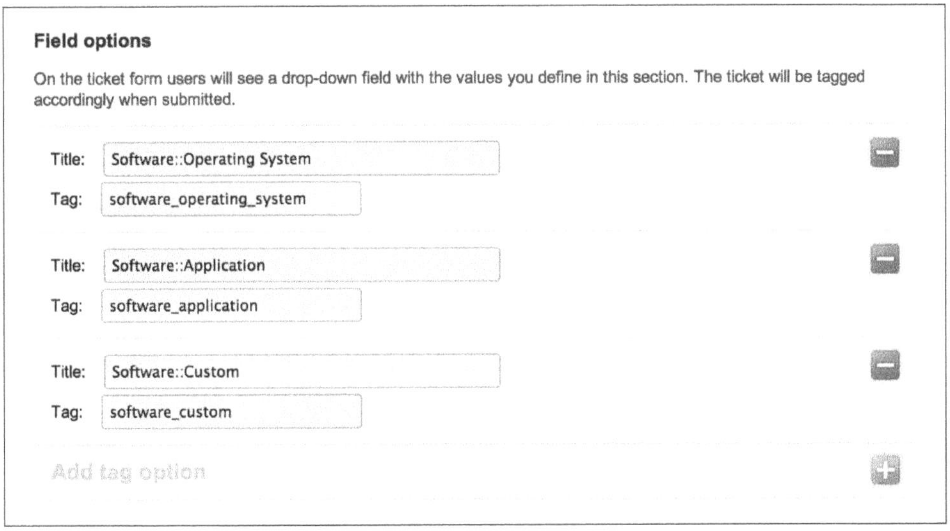

Field options

On the ticket form users will see a drop-down field with the values you define in this section. The ticket will be tagged accordingly when submitted.

Title:	Software::Operating System
Tag:	software_operating_system
Title:	Software::Application
Tag:	software_application
Title:	Software::Custom
Tag:	software_custom

Add tag option

Figure 6-7. Options in the drop-down list to configure a menu

When you're defining menus, the rule is that whenever :: appears and the text before two options is the same, everything before the :: will become a menu and everything after the :: is shown as the second level of the menu. For the Software menu described earlier, Figure 6-8 shows the result displayed to the user. In this screenshot, the first level of the menu is shown on the left, and the second level is shown on the right.

Figure 6-8. Result of configuring a menu of options (two screenshots shown side by side for convenience)

 If you're using this option and enabling custom fields on your Feedback tab (as described in "Creating a New Feedback Tab" on page 64), you should be aware that this drop-down-list menu will be flattened when displayed to the user, but only when displayed on the feedback tab.

Ordering Fields

The order in which the fields are listed to users will depend on the person viewing the page. As an administrator, you will have complete control over the order in which fields are presented to end users. You'll have less control over the order in which fields are presented to agents because the system fields have a predefined order.

The process to define the field order is simple: click the Reorder link on the Ticket fields administration page. This link will add boxes around each of the fields (see Figure 6-9), and you will be able to drag and drop each of the fields to the desired position. When you're finished, click the Done button.

When an agent views the ticket creation or edit page, the rules for the ordering fields are simple:

- List all of the system fields in their standard order.
- List all custom fields using the order defined for them by the administrator.

When an end user views the ticket creation page, the order of all fields will exactly match the order defined by the administrator, even if the custom fields have been positioned before any of the system fields.

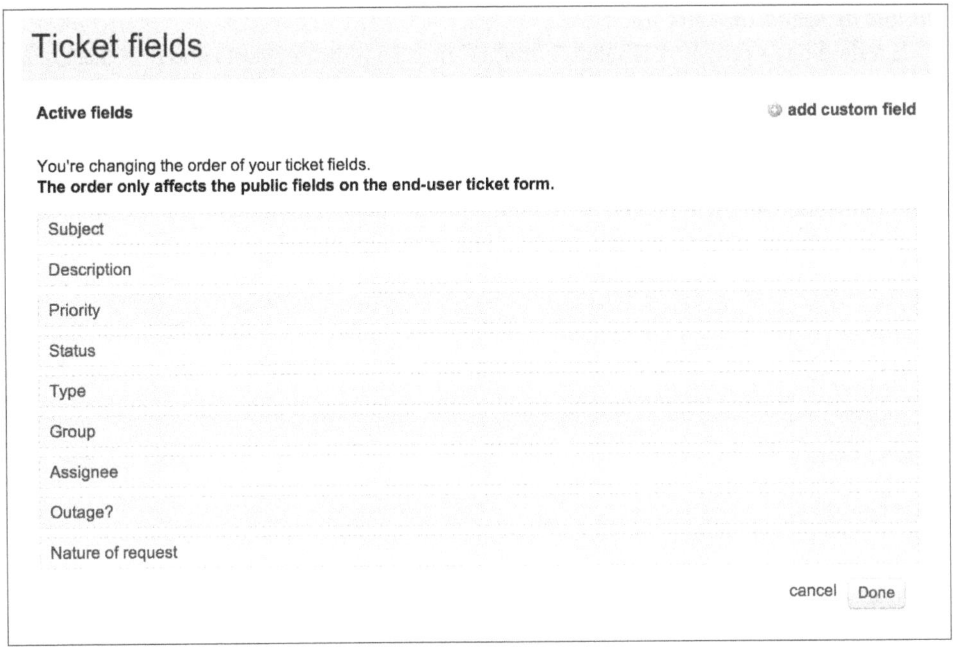

Ticket fields

Active fields   ⊕ add custom field

You're changing the order of your ticket fields.
The order only affects the public fields on the end-user ticket form.

Subject

Description

Priority

Status

Type

Group

Assignee

Outage?

Nature of request

                                                              cancel   Done

Figure 6-9. Drag-and-drop interface for reordering ticket fields

Reading the List of Ticket Fields

The configuration of each field, including the settings described in "End-User Fields" on page 89, is summarized beside each field on the "Ticket field" administration page. Figure 6-10 shows a sample set of fields in the leftmost "Active fields" column. The administrator's configuration choices are reflected as follows:

Field category
> The third column shows whether the field is a *System* or *Custom* field.

Visibility
> Fields that are shown to end users (Subject, Description, Assignee, and "Nature of request") have a gray box labeled "visible" next to them. Fields without this box (Priority, Status, Type, and Group) are visible to agents and administrators only. The "Outage?" field is visible to end users because they can edit it, as will be described shortly.

Required for agents
> An example of a field in the list that is required for agents is Assignee, which has an asterisk (*) beside the name of the field. Technically, the Description field is required for agents as well, but because it's implicit and not configurable, it is not noted on this screen.

Editable by agents and end users

If a field has a gray box labeled "editable" next to it, both agents and end users can change its contents.

Required for end users

The Subject, Description, and "Nature of request" fields in the screenshot meet this criterion, because they have both the word "editable" in the gray box beside the field name, and an asterisk to indicate that the field is required.

The rightmost "edit" column allows you to change the configuration of the field.

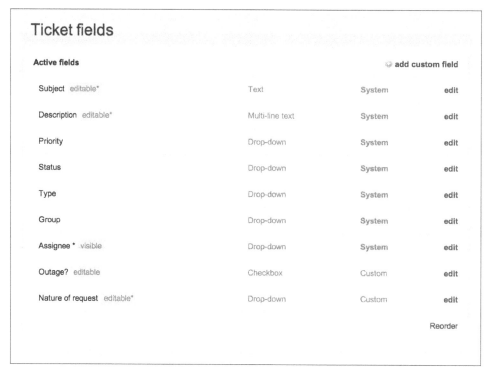

Figure 6-10. Configured set of ticket fields

Custom User and Organization Fields

Just as you can add custom fields to tickets, you can add custom fields to user and organization profiles. Unlike ticket fields, however, user and organization fields are visible to and can be used only by agents, not end users. The purpose of these custom fields is to track data about your customers that can then be used to segment them and create unique workflows. So, for example, if you decided to rank your customers by the amount they spend on your products or services and provide support based on that (the more they spend, the faster the response and resolution to support issues), you could add a custom field for monthly or yearly spending and pull the relevant data into this custom field via an API integration with the system that tracks this data.

All of your custom fields are available as conditions in your business rules. This means that you can create a support workflow that checks for these custom fields and then acts on the data contained within them. Using this example, if you were to create a custom user field called "Monthly spend," you could create a trigger that made an agent or group assignment or set the priority based on the amount of the monthly spend. Aside from the ability to route incoming tickets, merely having this data contained within a user or organization profile gives you much more detail about the customers you're providing support for. You can consider this one of the steps in bringing customer relationship management into your Zendesk instance.

Administrators create custom user and organization fields, and agents can see and use them. You'll see both the User Fields and Organization Fields administration pages in your Zendesk instance. Although the fields you create apply separately to each, the pages you use to create them are exactly the same. Like custom fields for tickets, you select a field type such as a drop-down, text, or checkbox and then fill in the details. Your custom fields are immediately available in user and organization profiles.

Custom user and organization fields are available on the Regular, Plus, and Enterprise plans, but not Starter.

Ticket Forms

In your Help Center, your customers can request support by filling out and submitting the "Submit a Request" form. As we explained in "Custom Fields" on page 104, you can create your own custom ticket fields and add them to this form. This allows you to collect more information about the customer's issue that you can then use to route the ticket to the appropriate group or agent.

In the Enterprise version of Zendesk, you can take this a big step further and dynamically display entirely different ticket forms to address different support needs. You could, for example, prompt the customer to first select the product he needs support for and then display a ticket form specifically for that product, or you might instead create ticket forms that reflect support workflows such as software versus hardware support.

Like custom fields, each ticket form can be visible to both agents and end users, or just to agents. Your first ticket form is called Default Ticket Form, and it's the one that is active and visible to your users before you create other ticket forms. It's there so that you have a ticket form to display to your end users in the Help Center. After you've created at least one more ticket form and make it active and visible to end users, your users will see the drop-down list of active forms and choose from that list.

Ticket forms are not supported in the Feedback tab. If you selected the "Display custom fields to end users" option on the Feedback channel administration page, all of the custom ticket fields that have been marked as visible to end users will be displayed in the Feedback tab. Until the Feedback tab does support ticket forms, you may want to turn that option off unless you want your customers to see all of your custom ticket fields.

Ticket forms are built in tandem with custom ticket fields, and each has its own administration page in your Zendesk instance. You'll find Ticket Forms right below Ticket Fields in the administration Manage menu. Start by clicking "Add form" on the Ticket Forms page, which displays a screen like the one in Figure 6-11.

The first input is for the name of the form. The name displayed to agents is on the left and the name displayed to end users is on the right and will be editable when you click the "Form name for end users" checkbox. Selecting this checkbox also makes the form visible to end users in the Help Center. Below the form name you'll see all the active system ticket fields. Those that are required are grayed out and cannot be removed from the form.

Figure 6-11. Editing a ticket form

The first input is for the name of the form. The name displayed to agents is on the left, and the name displayed to end users is on the right and will be editable when you click the "Form name for end users" checkbox. Selecting this checkbox also makes the form visible to end users in the Help Center. Below the form name, you'll see all the active system ticket fields. Those that are required are grayed out and cannot be removed from the form.

Your custom ticket fields are listed to the right of the system fields. If you've just created new custom ticket fields, you may need to refresh the page to see them. To add a custom ticket field to the form, simply drag and drop it into the list of ticket fields on the left. Your custom ticket fields will be added below the system ticket fields. You can reorder the custom ticket fields on the form by dragging and dropping them into a new position. You cannot, however, reorder the system fields.

After you've selected the custom ticket fields you want to add to this form, click "Save form." Follow this procedure and create as many ticket forms as needed. Figure 6-12 shows a ticket form for three example products, all of them visible to end users.

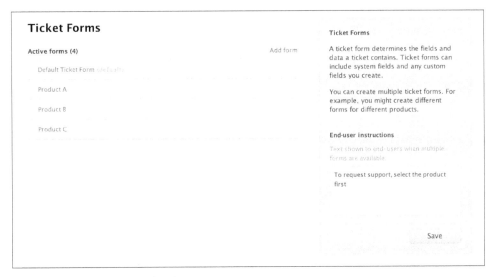

Figure 6-12. The list of ticket forms

If you need to edit any of your ticket forms, click the ticket form title. Unlike other administration pages, there is no "edit" link for the forms in the list. The final step is to add the text that prompts the end users to select a form. In Figure 6-12, we've entered "To request support, select the product first." After entering your end user instructions, click Save.

When your end users visit your Help Center and select "Submit a request," rather than seeing a form, they'll see a drop-down list that contains all of your active ticket forms that are visible to end users (Figure 6-13). When they select a form, it's displayed on the page, where they can fill it in and submit it.

Figure 6-13. How end users select the appropriate ticket form

You can directly link to a specific ticket form rather than sending your users to the "Submit a request" page. When your forms are active and visible to end users, go to the Help Center and click the "Submit a request" link. Select the ticket form from the drop-down list. In your browser's address bar, you'll see that the URL is appended with the ticket form ID; a typical URL is *https://blueskies.zendesk.com/hc/en-us/requests/new? ticket_form_id=12784.*

You can copy the entire URL and make it available to users (in email, for example). You can find the ticket ID by hovering your cursor over the ticket form name on the Ticket Forms administration page, but you'll need to put that ID into a URL that follows the example format shown.

The ticket forms you create can be used in search and in your views, automations, and triggers. If you wanted to route incoming tickets based on the product ticket form that was used, you can add a condition in a trigger. All of your ticket forms are available as both conditions and actions in automations and triggers. (These automated business rules are covered in Chapter 8.)

If you want to create views for each product-specific ticket form, you can add a ticket form as a condition in a view, as shown in Figure 6-14.

Figure 6-14. Using ticket forms in a view

CHAPTER 7

Agent Support Process

Zendesk is the kind of tool that allows you to create a new instance (without requiring any installation, because it's SaaS) and immediately start providing support to your customers. Out of the box, there are some nifty default settings that will assist with the process.

This is fine to start with, but as your business and support processes mature, it's a good idea to ensure that your Zendesk instance matures with them. Some of these processes are less tangible and will require user education only, but for the other tasks, you can use *macros* and *views* for business process automation. This chapter describes these tools, and some of the other techniques that your agents will use to support your customers.

Restricting Agent Access to Tickets

On the agent creation page, administrators can use the "Has access to" option to restrict what the agent can access. Most administrators elect to give all agents access to all tickets, which is the least restrictive of the options. We encourage you to select this option. The simple reason is that it allows agents to proactively find tickets that are new in your Zendesk instance, triage them, and possibly work on them. All of the other options would require an automatic triage policy to be set up (see "Triggers" on page 132), or a dedicated person to assign new tickets to agents manually. Assigning a team member to function as a triage manager is a potential roadblock, particularly if the person happens to be out of the office when an important ticket comes in, which adds potential risk to providing great customer service.

The option to restrict access to "Tickets within this agent's group(s)" means that the agent must wait for someone else to assign the ticket to his group before reading it (or even knowing it exists). Be aware that agents restricted in this way cannot view tickets that are waiting to be assigned to a group. The option "Tickets assigned to this agent only" takes this one step further and says that an agent can view only tickets that have been specifically assigned to him. This is the most restrictive access, and completely prevents agents from proactively finding new tickets and solving them.

The final option of "Tickets requested by users in this agent's organization" helps to preserve customer privacy. If you elect to use this option, it's important that you assign the agent to a customer organization in the Organization drop-down list on the agent creation page (see "Adding an Agent Account" on page 41 for further details). Agents restricted in this way cannot view tickets outside the organization to which they are assigned, and if you use this option for all agents, customers have the security of knowing that only a fixed, limited group of agents can ever see their tickets.

Presumptive Solve Approach

You must define many support processes up front in order to run a successful customer service program. Many of these process definitions will require user education, and cannot be automated in Zendesk.

One process we strongly encourage customers to adopt is the *presumptive solve approach*. Consider a scenario where a customer submits a ticket asking for a certain piece of information, and the agent replies to the ticket with the information that she believes answers the question. At this stage, the agent has the option of solving the ticket or leaving it in the Open status. The options can be analyzed as follows:

Leave the ticket open
    So as not to potentially offend the requester of the ticket, the agent might set the status of the ticket to Open. She does this because she's concerned that it's presumptuous of her to assume that she's already answered the customer's inquiry. If she did answer the question successfully, the customer might come back and say "thanks," but it's also very possible (more likely, in fact) that the customer won't reply at all. The agent won't know whether she has solved the request, and the ticket will be sitting in her queue every day until she hears back. At this stage, the agent can send a follow-up to the customer, to which the customer may or may not respond, or she can simply solve the ticket. Adopting this approach for your customer service workflow assumes that the customer is going to respond eventually to confirm that the ticket has been answered. Typically, this rarely occurs, and the agent is left with a situation where she needs to presumptively solve the ticket anyway.

Presumptively solve the ticket
    The alternative to the preceding approach is that when the agent provides the answer to the question in the ticket, she sets the status of the ticket to Solved immediately. This *might* seem presumptuous, but as discussed earlier in the "Ticket Status" on page 96, Zendesk will automatically reopen requests that were solved when a customer replies, so the customer still has a means of continuing the con-

versation with the agent. In other words, the customer could simply reply to request a better explanation from the agent, and the ticket will be immediately reopened. Adopting this support workflow will produce a cleaner database of tickets, and requires less effort from agents. The risk is that customers will be offended by the agent's presumption that she has answered the inquiry, but I've found that the benefit of adopting this policy outweighs this risk.

Another benefit of the presumptive solve approach is that the *resolution time* metric in Zendesk will accurately reflect the amount of time that the agent took to provide what she believed was the answer to the ticket. If your agents keep tickets open indefinitely until the customer responds, this metric won't accurately measure when tickets were solved. It will more accurately reflect the amount of time it took before the agent got frustrated with the lack of response and solved the ticket.

 If you or your support manager are concerned that agents are using the presumptive solve approach and typically not answering customer inquiries properly in their first response, Zendesk has some metrics that can help you to measure this. If you are on the Plus or Enterprise plans and have linked Zendesk with GoodData, you can analyze the *Reopens* and *Replies* metrics. Using this data allows you to balance the workflow and ensure that your agents are adopting just the right amount of "presumption."

Views

When a support agent opens Zendesk every morning, she somehow needs to find the tickets that she should be answering that day. The feature that allows her to do this is called *views*. These can simply be described as "saved searches." When you create a view, you're defining the conditions for the search. The view does not save the search results themselves. Often, agents will create their own views (and are able to do so, if you are on the Regular, Plus, or Enterprise plans). We encourage Zendesk customers to let their agents create their own views, but we also strongly encourage administrators to work with support managers to find out which views should be created as a standard baseline for agents. Standardizing a set of views for all agents will provide a a consistent and reliable process for your agents to follow. Beyond that, minor changes by agents are fine.

I generally find that the default views in Zendesk are useful for organizations just getting started. As your setup matures, you can modify these views to reflect your customized use of the product. For example, if you are getting 100 tickets every hour and would like to use the "Recently updated tickets" more effectively, you might change one criterion in this view to show tickets from the past 2 hours, instead of the past 24 hours.

Aside from creating new views, administrators really only have one setting in Zendesk to configure for views. On the Tickets administration page, there is an option labeled

Views with a checkbox labeled "List empty views." By default, when an agent clicks the toolbar icon to display her views, Zendesk will include every view in the list, even if the view is empty. In this case, empty views will appear in a lighter gray color. If your Zendesk instance has a large number of views, this can be a poor use of screen real estate. If this is the case, you can deselect the "List empty views" checkbox on the Tickets administration page, which will cause empty views never to be listed for agents.

To get started with creating views, you'll need to open the Views management page and click the "add view" link. The following sections show you how to handle each part of the dialog presented to you.

Definition of Current User

As you're defining your process in views, macros, and triggers, you'll probably notice the phrase *current user* scattered throughout the options. To summarize what this means, the current user is *the user who is executing the action.*

In the context of a macro, the current user will be the agent who clicked the link to apply the macro. In the context of a view, the current user is the person who is reading the list of tickets in the view. In the context of a trigger, the current user is the person who made the change on the ticket, which resulted in the trigger being fired.

Automations do not refer to the current user in their configuration, because automations are fired by Zendesk itself, not as a result of an action by any individual person.

Understanding View Conditions

Every view has two types of conditions:

All conditions

> Every condition in this set must be met by the list of tickets in the results. For instance, if this section contains one condition that the Status must be Open and another condition that the Priority must be High, the only results shown by this view will be the open tickets with a high priority.

Any conditions

> One or more of the conditions in this section must be met, but it is not necessary for all of the conditions to be met. For instance, if one condition in this section says that the Group must be Sales and another condition says that the Group must be Finance, the results will include all tickets that are assigned to the Sales group, in

addition to all tickets assigned to the Finance group. Because every ticket can be assigned only to one group at a time, it would be impossible for a ticket to be assigned to both of these groups anyway. So having this particular condition in the "Any conditions" section is necessary to be able to achieve this set of search results.

An example of these conditions is shown in Figure 7-1, which uses two "All conditions" to find unsolved tickets assigned to the current user, and also uses two "Any conditions" to find all tickets from Zendesk Voice.

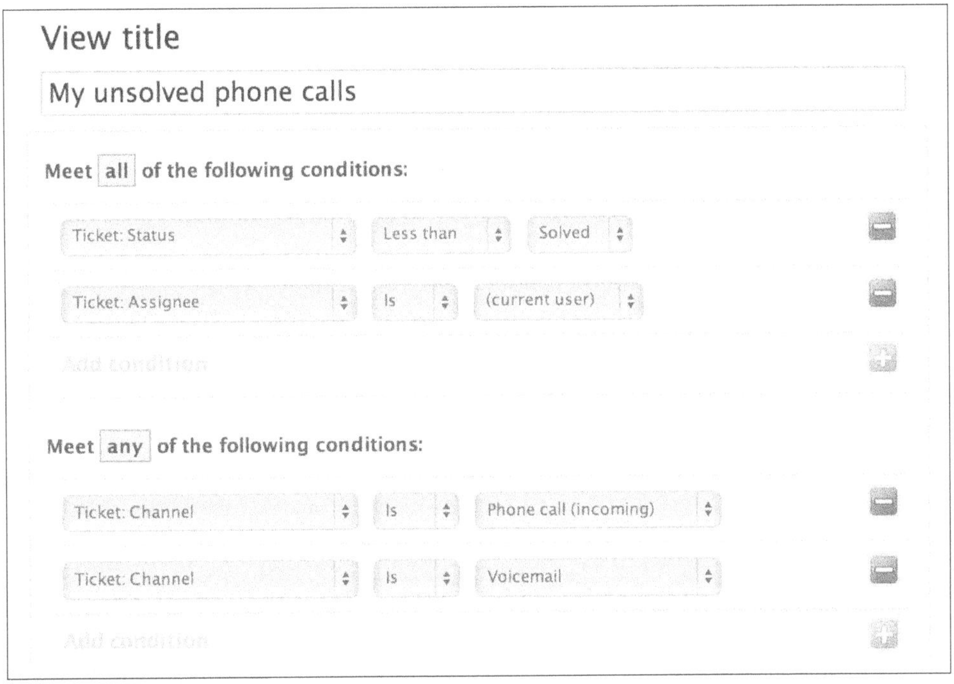

Figure 7-1. Example conditions for a view

After you've selected your relevant set of conditions, you can test the view by clicking the "Preview match for the conditions above" button.

When you create a condition, you'll often have the option to select three drop-down lists: the field, the qualifier, and the value. The qualifiers "is" and "is not" are simple, but in the case of the qualifiers "less than" or "greater than," it's not necessarily obvious what is considered less or more. The rule is this: *less than* refers to everything above the selected item in the drop-down list. For example, in the Status field, everything *above* the Solved status includes New, Open, and Pending. *Greater than* refers to everything below the selected item in the drop-down list. For example, in the Priority field, everything *below* Normal includes the options High and Urgent.

Required Fields for Views

When you're creating views, you might occasionally get an error message that says:

> *Status less than solved has been added as a hidden rule because at least one of the following ticket properties are required in the ALL conditions section: Status, Type, Group, Assignee, or Requester*

Basically, this message is telling you that every view must contain at least one condition that checks one of these five fields. The reason for this is purely technical: the way that databases work is that they *index* data before searching. In order for this indexing process to work very quickly, only certain types of fields—usually numerical fields—can be indexed. The five fields mentioned in the error message are the ones that Zendesk uses to index the data, so it's necessary that at least one of the fields appears in every view. Otherwise, your views would take a considerable amount of time to execute, would produce a significant strain on the Zendesk servers, and no one wins.

To satisfy this requirement, you should almost always add a condition to check that the status of a ticket is less than solved. If you'd like to include solved and/or closed tickets, then you could also use a condition that checks for all tickets of a certain type. Most of the time it's not really an inconvenience, unless you see the error message and you don't understand what it means because you haven't read this section of the book.

 This message will also be displayed to agents who are creating their own views, so be prepared to explain this section to your agents when it happens.

View Formatting Options

Views are displayed in a table format, and you have the option of modifying which columns are shown and how the ticket data is organized. The selection of fields included in the table can be fully customized by the creator of the view (via drag-and-drop), as shown in Figure 7-2.

You also have the option of grouping the tickets together, in addition to ordering them. You can use this feature to group all tickets by priority, then order them by request date. The result is that all Urgent priority tickets will appear first, then the High priority tickets, and so on. When the settings in this example (shown in Figure 7-3) are applied, even if a ticket was requested a year ago, if it has an Urgent priority it will appear above a High priority ticket requested last week.

Formatting options	Table columns
	Drag and drop to select and reorder columns in your table. You can add a total of 9 columns to a table.

Columns not included in table | Columns included in table

Columns not included in table	Columns included in table
ID	Subject
Latest update by requester	Request date
Submitter	Requester
Assigned date	Ticket type
Latest update by assignee	Priority

Figure 7-2. Using drap-and-drop to add or remove colums from a view

Group by

Priority   ⬍   ⦿ Ascending   ○ Descending

Order by

Request date   ⬍   ○ Ascending   ⦿ Descending

Figure 7-3. Grouping and ordering options when editing a view

Shared Views

Agents on the Regular, Plus, and Enterprise plans can create views for personal use. Administrators on all plans can configure the standard set of views available for all agents, and administrators on the Plus and Enterprise plans can create views that are shared with a specific group of agents. Administrators on the Enterprise plan can also grant the privilege of creating shared views to agents, which is explained in "Configuration Options for Agent Roles" on page 44. The ability to grant agents the privilege of sharing views is one of our favorite features of the Zendesk Enterprise plan.

After following the instructions in "Understanding View Conditions" on page 120 to set the conditions for your view and defining the format of the results, you'll see a section at the bottom of the view creation page labeled "Available for" (as shown in Figure 7-4). This section allows you to create a *shared view*, as opposed to a *personal view*. The sharing options allow you to share the view with all users or to share it with a single group. If you'd like to share the same view with two groups, such as Level 2 Support and Level 3 Support, a workaround would be to create a new group named Higher Level Support, add all of the agents from both groups, and then share the view with that one group.

Figure 7-4. Options for creating shared and personal views

After you've created some shared views, you'll be able to filter the list of views on the Views management page by clicking the drop-down list marked "All shared views" and selecting a specific group instead. When updated, this page will show only the views that have been shared with the selected group, allowing you to audit the shared views more easily.

The option to share the view with "All agents" will be selected automatically when you create a new view as an administration. If you opened this page to create a new view for personal use only, it's important that you change the sharing option to be "Me only." Otherwise, everyone will see the new view in the list.

Macros

Every customer service team, regardless of how it supports its customers, will find that there are a few questions customers ask over and over again. Every time this question is added, the agents must write the same or similar answer for the customer. To make this process more efficient, Zendesk has a feature named *macros* that allows agents to define actions that they can repeat by simply clicking a couple of links, or using keyboard shortcuts.

Just like views, macros will often be defined by the agents who use them. After all, your agents are the people who understand their process best. But as with views, it's also possible for an administrator to define a standard baseline set of macros. Unfortunately, it's very difficult to predict the types of questions that you'll get from your customers, or the tasks that your agents will be performing over and over again. As an administrator, you should start with very few macros. You can then speak to your agents about the personal macros they find most useful, and create shared versions of these macros that are available to all other agents.

Unlike views, the default Zendesk macros are not particularly useful and are mostly for demonstration purposes. That's OK, though, because if you educate your users on the process of creating macros, hopefully you'll start to see some really useful macros appearing quickly. If you're on the Enterprise plan, you will also be able to give your agents the permissions to share macros with other agents directly.

Adding a Shared Macro

Just like with views, all administrators can create macros that are shared only with all agents, but if you're on the Plus and Enterprise plans, you can also add new macros that are shared with specific groups. Macros are added from the Macros management page in Zendesk. The first tab on this page lists the *Shared Macros* and the second tab lists your *Personal Macros*. As an administrator, you're not likely to have your own personal macros, because most of the time, administrators don't solve support requests (although there are situations where this does happen). To get started with macro creation, click the "add macro" like in the upper-right corner of this page.

Every macro must have a title, and at least one action. Among the available actions is the ability to update the values of all fields, including system and custom fields. We won't explain all of the fields here because they are mostly intuitive, but there are a few options in the list of actions that sometimes confuse people:

"Set subject"
> This option will erase the existing subject of a ticket and replace it with the value set in the macro. There is currently no way to suffix or prefix the subject with a piece of text.

Difference between "set tags" and "add tags"
> The difference is quite simple: "set tags" will remove the existing tags and replace them with the tags defined in the macro, whereas "add tags" keeps the current tags and adds new tags as defined in the macro. To be honest, I've never seen a valid use for the "set tags" option. Because it comes first, we often hear from customers that they select this option accidentally, and then they are frustrated to find that the existing tags on the ticket are erased when the macro is executed. So it's important that you don't make the same mistake, and remember to choose "add tags" unless, for whatever reason, you need to erase all of the current tags on the ticket.

Separate options for "Comment/description" and "Comment mode"
> When an agent adds a comment to a ticket from the ticket screen, he'll have the option to mark the comment as *private*. The process of adding a comment and setting its visibility probably seems like a single step to the agent, but technically, the agent has changed two fields: the comment text and the comment mode. On macros when you add an action to publish a comment, these fields are presented separately, and are named *Comment/description* and *Comment mode*. Sometimes you'll want your macro to add a comment to the ticket without explicitly setting the visibility mode, in which case the comment will use the existing visibility setting on the ticket. In other cases, you might want to change the comment visibility without adding a comment at all. For example, if your macro was assigning a ticket

internally, the comment mode should be set to private, without necessarily adding the comment text in the macro. This is the reason that these fields are separate in the macro configuration screen.

After you've defined the set of actions for your macro, you can share the macro in the same way that you share a view, which is described in "Shared Views" on page 123. Similar to views, macros can be shared with all agents, or just a specific group.

 With the exception of macros that provide a set of instructions in the form of a comment, my general rule is that the ideal number of actions in a macro is three. Any less than this, and the macro doesn't do much (with a few exceptions, such as tagging with difficult words). Any more than three actions, and the macro is so specific that it's hard to find a relevant situation in which you would use it.

Macro Menus

As the number of macros increases in your Zendesk instance, it can be difficult for your agents to navigate a long list of macros to find the ones that are most important. The feature to create *macro menus* assists with this, by allowing you to define multiple cascading levels in your macros. The syntax for this function is exactly the same as the syntax described in "Cascading Menus in Drop-Down Lists" on page 107.

It's surprisingly simple to use this feature. Just add two colons (`::`) in the macro at the point where the menu break should occur. Everything that appears before the `::` in the macro name will be used as the menu name, and everything after the `::` is considered the second level. It's possible to use this technique several times in the same macro to create multiple menus.

In Figure 7-5, we defined two macros that have a primary menu of "Take it," then a secondary set of options to assign a priority. I could have extended the first option to create a third level by naming the macro `Take it::with normal priority::and make incident`, which is a macro with three different cascading levels.

The macros from this example will be presented to the agent in the menu format shown in Figure 7-6 (the first level of the menu is shown on the left, and the second level is shown on the right).

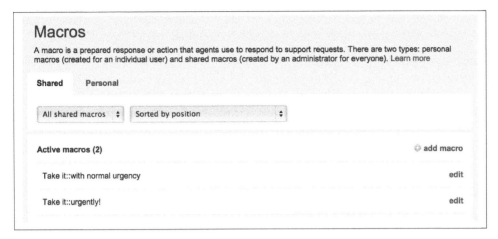

Figure 7-5. *Definition of a macro menu on the Macro management page*

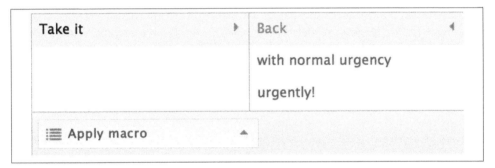

Figure 7-6. *Macro menu shown to the agent (screenshot modified and shown side by side for convenience)*

There are many different scenarios in which you might want to use this feature:

Defining next steps

You might use a macro similar to the default "Take it!" macro, which immediately assigns a ticket to the agent who executes the macro. It's possible to set the first level of the menu to the text "Take it," then have the second level define the next steps, such as assigning a priority to the ticket. This is the example just shown.

Categorizing for agent convenience

To illustrate this idea, suppose you have a dedicated group of agents who have the responsibility of managing social media tickets in your Zendesk instance. You'll probably define a convenient set of macros for them to use. Rather than asking the social media team to navigate through the same long list of macros as every other agent, you might use a macro menu to create a "Social media" first-level menu, and then all of the social media macros would be included on the second level.

Funneling into the correct action
If you have several business processes defined to escalate tickets under various circumstances, it's possible to create menus to make the process simpler. Your first-level menu could be Escalate, and your second-level menus might be Supervisors, Level 2 Support, or another group at your organization. In other words, the sentence is being completed by the combination of the selected levels in the macro menu. This also saves space compared to the alternative option of listing all of the different escalation groups in the first level of the macro menu.

Referring Macros to the Knowledge Base

If you're planning to use macros to provide detailed step-by-step instructions to customers (and most organizations do), you should take advantage of the Help Center feature in Zendesk (see Chapter 9). As an example, let's assume that you're providing a set of instructions to change a user's password. Instead of the instructions being included in the macro itself, the best practice is for the macro to refer to instructions in a knowledge base article. There are a few reasons for this:

Maintenance
Because it's impossible to update the fields of a closed ticket, it would be impossible to update the instructions if the process to change a password changed. The steps might be valid at the time that they were given to the customer, but if the steps change afterward and the customer revisits the ticket, the instructions will be out of date.

Encouraging self-service
By linking the ticket to a knowledge base article, you're effectively making the customer aware of the existence of your Zendesk Help Center, and the extensive set of FAQs that you've (hopefully) published there. Next time the customer needs a simple question answered, she might go check the FAQs before submitting a new ticket to your support team.

Search engine optimization
By having the instructions listed in your knowledge base, you make it possible for Google and other search engines to include the instructions in search results. Before your customers even have the chance to submit a ticket, they might use their search engine to find the answer, and your knowledge base article might provide the answer to them immediately.

If you're linking to a knowledge base article in a macro or a comment, you might notice that the URL looks like *https://mycompany.zendesk.com/hc/en-us/articles/200204449-How-do-I-customize -my-Help-Center-*. The section of the URL that says "-How-do-I-customize-my-Help-Center-" is technically redundant, and you can link to *https://mycompany.zendesk.com/hc/en-us/articles/200204449* (or the equivalent in your Zendesk instance) instead, which is the same URL without the full title of the article. This is all that's required for the URL to work. The title is ignored. This means that if you did happen to use the full URL that includes the title of the article in a macro and you at some point change the title without updating the URL that's contained in a macro, the URL will still work.

CHAPTER 8

Automated Business Rules

Every organization has a slightly different set of ideas for how it would like to support customers. When we have implemented Zendesk solutions for organizations, support managers sometimes said they had a "standard customer service setup," but over the years we've learned that there is no such thing. When we really dug into what each support manager wanted to accomplish with Zendesk, we found that the requirements were quite specific to the particular organization, as each one has a unique set of circumstances that impact how Zendesk should be set up.

In order to accommodate this diverse range of customer requirements, Zendesk offers a very flexible set of tools to capture your organization's business process. In the previous chapter, we explained views and macros, which are the first pieces of your business process, but dealt with them from the agent's perspective.

From an administrator's perspective, you can define a number of automated business rules using *triggers* and *automations*. This chapter will describe each of these in detail, along with some other business rules that may be configured by administrators in Zendesk.

User and Organization Tagging

The *User and Organization Tagging* feature is one of our personal favorites in Zendesk, because it's so simple, but makes it so much easier for you to provide varying levels of support to each of your customers. Using this feature, administrators can add tags to users or organizations in the same way that an agent might add a tag to a ticket. Then when an end user submits a ticket, that ticket inherits the tags from the end user's profile, or the organization to which he is linked. An example use of this feature would be to tag a user as a "vip" or his organization as having the "premier_support" package. In "Tags" on page 101, we described tags as the glue that connects business rules, and this is a good example. You might use the "vip" user tag to define an automated rule that raises the priority of tickets from all VIP customers if their ticket has not been solved within 48 hours.

This feature is disabled by default, but you can enable it by clicking the "Tags on users and organizations" checkbox on the Customers administration page.

Once this feature is enabled, you'll notice that every time you edit a user's profile, it will include a Tags field. You might also notice that whenever you create or edit an organization, the Tags field also appears. This field works in the same way as the Tags field on tickets—when you enter some text and press the space bar, the tag is added in its own box. Once you're finished adding tags, you can just navigate away from the page because changes are saved automatically.

To find a list of users or organizations with a specific tag, you can click the "tags" link on the People management page, which will show a report of all tags added, and the list of users and organizations associated with each tag.

 It's possible to add tags to agent and administrator user profiles, but this is less useful than adding tags to end users because agents and administrators generally don't submit tickets. It can be very useful in the context of configuring the visibility of sections in the Help Center, though, which is covered in "Section Access Restrictions" on page 161.

Immediately after you add the tags to a user or organization, those tags will be inherited by new tickets created by that user. The tags are not applied retroactively to tickets, but if you need to do this, you can perform a search for all tickets submitted by a specific requester and perform a bulk update. The bulk update operation inside views will add the specified tags as new tags on the tickets, without removing the existing tags.

The user and organization tagging feature is really just the first step in a mature business process. In the next section on triggers and the subsequent one on automations (on page 140), we'll explain some of the uses for tags on tickets, which will highlight the value for you.

Triggers

Triggers are configurable actions that will be fired when an event occurs. As an administrator, you can use triggers to turn your business process into business rules in Zendesk. The best way to explain triggers is to provide examples on how to use them, which will be the approach in this section of the book.

Default Triggers

Triggers can be added and customized by administrators from the Triggers administration page. Eight triggers are activated by default in Zendesk, each of which provides some value to most organizations. These default triggers can be grouped into three categories:

Email notifications to the requester
> Whenever a ticket is updated with an important piece of information, the requester of the ticket—who is usually an end user—will receive an email notification with details of the update. There are three triggers in this category: one to notify the requester when the ticket is created, another one for when a ticket is updated with a comment, and one when the ticket is solved. These are the three big events in the life of the ticket, so they warrant a notification to the requester. It's important to note that the requester will not be notified when a field is changed without the addition of a comment, or when the added comment is marked as private. In other words, when your agents change the ticket status from New to Open, the customer will not be notified unless the agent adds a comment at the same time. It may be possible for the end user to sign into the Help Center to find out the new status, though.

Email notifications to the assignee
> When an update is made to a ticket, the agent working on that ticket should receive an email notification about the change. This might encourage the agent to sign into your Zendesk instance and add another update to the ticket. By default, the three events that are important to an assignee are when a comment is added to the ticket, when a ticket is assigned to her, and when the ticket is reopened. There is a default trigger that will send an email notification to the ticket assignee in each one of these situations.

Email notifications to all agents
> There are two default triggers in this category, the purpose of which are to notify a broad range of agents about new tickets. One of the triggers will notify all agents when a ticket is created without being assigned to a group, and the other trigger will notify just a specific group when the ticket is assigned to that group.

We occasionally hear from customers that the third category of triggers generates too many email notifications to agents, so they deactivate them. We've also worked with customers who disable the second category of default triggers, because they would prefer their agents to work inside Zendesk full-time, instead of working in email and waiting for email notifications to be sent to them. We rarely see situations in which the first category of default triggers is removed, because sending emails to your customers when a comment is added to their tickets is your best method of keeping them updated. Ultimately, each of these decisions should be made according to what is best for your organization, and the culture of email within your team.

Although the effect of all the default triggers is to send email notifications to someone, it's important to note that triggers can be used for many other purposes. The upcoming section "Trigger Examples" on page 135 has a number of triggers that do not send email notifications at all.

There's one more default trigger in Zendesk that is hard to notice, because it's deactivated by default. This trigger is named "Auto-assign to first email responding agent." The simple idea behind this trigger is that when a new ticket is created and an agent replies to the email notification saying something like "Got it!", the ticket will be automatically assigned to that agent. One potential issue with this process is that the agent's reply would be sent to the end user, unless the agent has used the correct email syntax to mark an email response as private. In general, it's also not a good practice to let agents pick tickets by email, because there might be someone better equipped at that time to take the ticket, who is signed into Zendesk directly. Those are the reasons that the trigger is deactivated by default.

Trigger Conditions and Actions

To start creating your own triggers, click the "add trigger" link in the upper-right corner of the Triggers administration page.

If you've already read "Views" on page 119, you'll be familiar with the format of trigger conditions. Just like views, trigger conditions have an *All* and an *Any* section. The conditions in the first section must all be met by all tickets in order for the trigger to be executed, and one or more of the conditions in the second section must be met by the tickets. The difference between the trigger and view conditions is that there are more options in the list of conditions that can be configured for triggers.

The first step when configuring any trigger is to decide if you would like the trigger to be executed on tickets that are created, or tickets that are updated. The latter does not include tickets that are created. To add the condition, select "Ticket is…" from the list of conditions, and select either "created" or "updated" from the list of options. If you would like the trigger to be executed on tickets are created *and* updated, you can exclude this condition from the trigger entirely.

After you've defined the complete set of conditions for your trigger, the next step is to define the actions that will occur on the tickets that meet the specified conditions. This part is similar to "Macros" on page 124, with some special actions such as "Requester language" added. As with macros, you can add as many actions as necessary to the trigger.

Trigger Examples

There are literally thousands of possible triggers that you could define in your Zendesk instance. Of those possible triggers, we see many consistent themes, but rarely are the business processes of two organizations exactly the same. The beauty of Zendesk's flexible triggering system is that you can customize your triggers to match however you want to achieve your customer support objectives. This section provides some example triggers, which you can either use verbatim in your instance, or customize for your specific use of the product.

Assign email ticket to the sales team

In "Incoming Email" on page 58, we explained that it's possible to create several incoming email addresses for your organization, such as *support@blueskies.com* and *sales@blueskies.com*, and have all of these addresses forward emails into your Zendesk instance. When the ticket is created, it's also possible to use triggers to automatically assign it to a specific team, based on the email address used by the customer. To configure this trigger, set the conditions as shown in Figure 8-1, and the actions as shown in Figure 8-2.

Figure 8-1. Conditions for the "Assign email ticket to sales team" trigger

Figure 8-2. Actions for the "Assign email ticket to sales team" trigger

Assign twickets to social media team

In the topics covered in "Twitter" on page 69, we explained that tickets created from Twitter are sensitive by nature, because the conversation can be easily broadcast to the world. For this reason, it might be worth immediately assigning all new twickets to your social media team to provide a response. To configure this trigger, set the conditions as shown in Figure 8-3, and the actions as shown in Figure 8-4.

Trigger title

Assign Twitter tickets to social media team

Meet all of the following conditions:

| Ticket: Is... | | Created |

Meet any of the following conditions:

Ticket: Channel		Is		Twitter
Ticket: Channel		Is		Twitter DM
Ticket: Channel		Is		Twitter Favorite

Figure 8-3. Conditions for the "Assign Twitter tickets to social media team" trigger

Perform these actions:

| Ticket: Group | | Social Media Support |

Figure 8-4. Actions for the "Assign Twitter tickets to social media team" trigger

Notify managers of urgent tickets

Whenever a ticket is given a priority of Urgent, it's obvious that a serious issue needs to be addressed. It's possible to write a trigger that would send an email alert to the people managing your team whenever a ticket is updated with this priority. Note that this trigger should be executed regardless of whether the ticket was created or updated, so there is no "Ticket is…" condition included in the trigger. Note also that the qualifier for the condition is "Changed to," which is necessary to ensure that the actions are executed only once, and not every time that the urgent ticket is updated. To configure this trigger, set the conditions as shown in Figure 8-5 and the actions as shown in Figure 8-6.

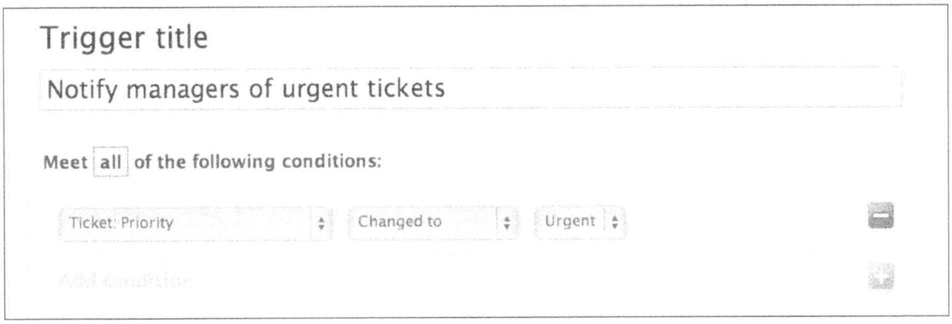

Figure 8-5. Conditions for the "Notify managers of urgent tickets" trigger

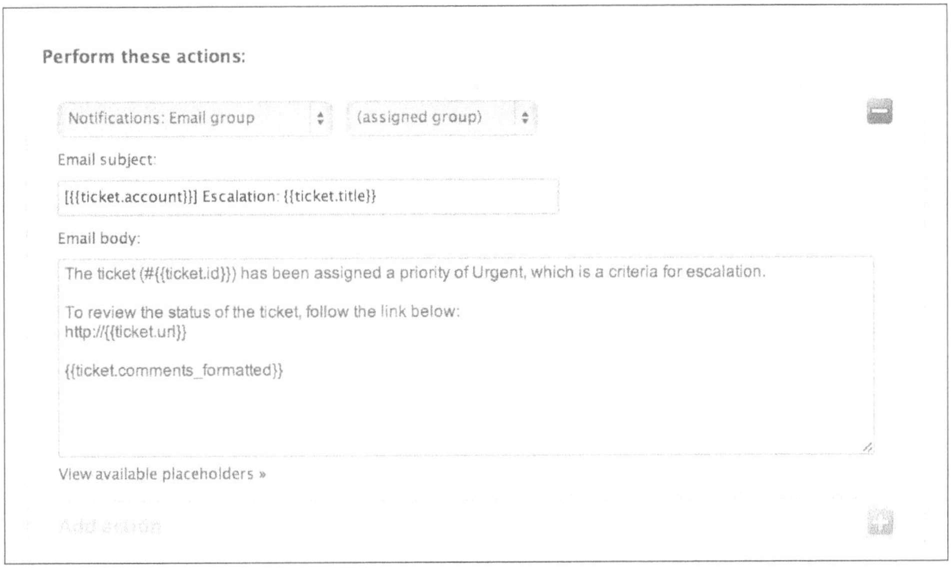

Figure 8-6. Actions for the "Notify managers of urgent tickets" trigger

Increase priority of tickets with the word "outage"
There is a slight trick to this trigger, because you might notice that there are no conditions to check the subject or description of a ticket. There is a condition to

check the "Comment text," though. What this condition really means is that it checks the comment text, but if the trigger was fired when a new ticket was added, technically the description is the comment text, so the condition will check the text in the Description field. Regardless, the text in the subject will also be checked every time this condition is run. This is very useful when you want to find a specific word such as *outage* in incoming emails or tickets. The other condition in this trigger, which checks that the action was executed by an end user, is useful to ensure that the trigger is not fired if the agent makes a casual comment such as "can you confirm if there is an outage?" to the requester. The conditions specified in this trigger will ensure that it is fired only when a customer makes a comment about the outage. To configure this trigger, set the conditions as shown in Figure 8-7 and the actions as shown in Figure 8-8.

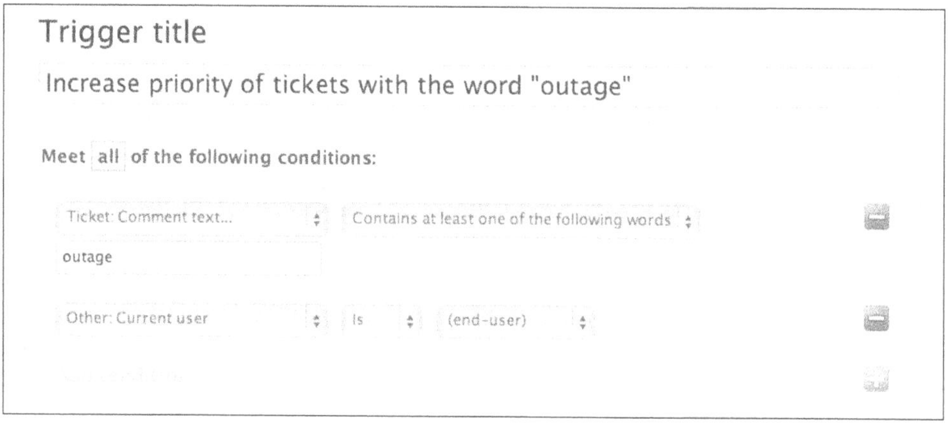

Figure 8-7. Conditions for the "Increase priority of tickets with the word outage" trigger

Figure 8-8. Actions for the "Increase priority of tickets with the word outage" trigger

Ordering Triggers

The order of triggers is important, because whenever a ticket is updated, the triggers will be executed in the order in which they are listed on the Triggers administration page. Many administrators make the mistake of ordering triggers for convenience or priority, but if you don't order your triggers appropriately, your processes may not work as you intended.

A good example concerns the default trigger "Notify all agents of received request" and the trigger "Assign email ticket to sales team" (discussed in detail in "Trigger Examples" on page 135). The default trigger "Notify all agents of received request" checks to see whether the ticket is assigned to a group, and if it's not assigned to a group, an email notification will be sent to all agents in your Zendesk instance. If this trigger appears at the top of the list, it will be one of the first triggers to be executed, and all agents will receive an email. If the "Assign email ticket to sales team" trigger was further down the list, it would assign tickets to the sales team when the conditions are met. This, in turn, would fire the email notification defined in the trigger "Notify group of assignment," the end result of which would send two email notifications to the sales team—one for the creation of the ticket, and another one for the assignment of a ticket. You'll also end up with a number of agents who receive an email about a ticket that was immediately assigned to a team for completion, meaning that the email notification was just unnecessary noise.

 Sending multiple emails to the same person for a single event is bad practice, because users will start to feel like they are being spammed with redundant notifications and will tune out the emails coming from Zendesk.

Fortunately, avoiding this situation is quite simple. On the Triggers administration page, you can select the link labeled Reorder. This will immediately add boxes around each of the triggers in the list, and using drag-and-drop, you can change the order of these triggers. In the example just discussed, you would move the trigger "Assign email ticket to sales team" to the top of the list, then the triggers "Notify all agents of received request" and "Notify group of assignment" further down the list. When a new ticket is created, it will be assigned to the sales team by the first trigger first (assuming that the conditions are met); then, an email will be sent directly to the sales team via the "Notify group of assignment" trigger, and the "Notify all agents of received request" trigger will not be executed because the conditions will not be met.

 Automations will also run in the order in which they are listed on the Automations management page. However, automations do not take action on a ticket until all automations are checked, which differs from triggers. How automations are run on your tickets is covered in detail in this Zendesk knowledge base article (*http://bit.ly/automations*).

Mutually Exclusive Triggers

Aside from ordering triggers appropriately to prevent multiple email notifications from being sent to users, you can also use *mutual exclusivity* to ensure that multiple emails are not sent for the same event, regardless of the trigger order. Triggers defined as mutually exclusive cannot possibly both be executed as a result of the same event.

Out of the box, Zendesk has a good example of mutually exclusive triggers. To see it, start by opening the "Notify requester of comment update" trigger. When you look at the conditions of this trigger, you'll notice that one of the conditions prevents the trigger from being fired when the status of the ticket is set to Solved. In other words, if someone adds a comment and solves the ticket, the customer would not be notified. That might seem unusual, because this is the exact situation in which it's very important to notify the customer.

The reason for this particular condition is that it prevents the trigger from overlapping with another trigger, named "Notify requester of solved request." The dedicated purpose of the latter trigger is to send an email notification to the customer when the ticket is solved, and this trigger contains a custom email template that notifies the customer explicitly that his request has been solved.

If the first trigger did not have the condition that prevents it from overlapping with the latter trigger, the customer would receive one email saying that a comment had been added to his ticket, and another email saying that his ticket has been solved. These duplicate emails are what mutually exclusive triggers help you to avoid.

Automations

Automations are very similar to triggers, but instead of being executed when an event occurs, an automation will be fired after a certain amount of time passes. Automations are also configured with a set of *All* conditions and a set of *Any* conditions, so many of the concepts to configure automations will already be familiar to you. For the same reasons as in the triggers section, we'll explain automations by example.

Automations are checked exactly once per hour (within a window of a few minutes), which means that the actions defined in an automation may not be applied until nearly an hour after the conditions in the automation are met. The automations are not necessarily run at the top of the hour, and it may not be exactly one hour between executions of an automation. In most situations, such as email reminders, this is not a serious issue, but in the case of service-level agreements (SLAs) with fine-grained definitions over the amount of time before a ticket is escalated, it can be more serious. You'll need to consider this limitation before writing your automations.

Default Automations

All automations in Zendesk are listed on the Automations administration page. On a completely fresh instance of Zendesk, only one automation is enabled by default. As you start to enable other features such as the Twitter channel, Facebook channel, and Customer Satisfaction, some other automations will be automatically created. There are also two default automations that are deactivated by default, but I encourage most administrators to activate them. They are named "Pending notification 24 hours" and "Pending notification 5 days," and are explained with the other default automations next.

Close ticket 4 days after status is set to solved

In "Ticket Status" on page 96, we explained that it's impossible for a person to manually change the status of a ticket to Closed by selecting the option in the ticket field. The only way to move a ticket into the Closed status is to use either this automation or one like it. It's possible to change this automation to allow a greater period of time than four days to reopen a ticket, but four days is usually an appropriate length of time, because the momentum of a ticket is usually lost after four days anyway. If you get a lot of complaints from customers that their tickets are closed too quickly and they'd like to be able to have a week or more to reopen them, you can update the conditions of this automation. Note that even if this automation is deleted or deactivated, Zendesk will wait a maximum of 28 days before automatically closing all tickets in the Solved status. This is built into the product and impossible to change.

Request customer satisfaction rating

If you've enabled the Customer Satisfaction feature (covered on page 151) on your Zendesk instance, this automation will be added for you automatically. The purpose of this automation is to send an email to the requester of a ticket exactly 24 hours after the ticket is solved, to ask her for her feedback. The format and contents of that email are defined in this automation, so most of the text can be customized, with the exception of the customer satisfaction question itself. If you feel that 24 hours is too soon to ask the customer for her feedback, you can change the timeframe in this automation. Just be aware that end users cannot submit customer satisfaction feedback on a closed ticket, so if the email is sent after one day, the customer has another three days to provide feedback before the ticket is closed by the previously described automation. If you extend the delay for the customer satisfaction email, you should change the closure automation as well. We also don't recommend sending the customer satisfaction email *immediately* after solving a ticket, because in some cases the agent will solve a ticket but the customer will have more questions (refer back to "Presumptive Solve Approach" on page 118 for more information on this). If an email was sent to the customer every time the ticket was solved to ask for her satisfaction feedback, it could very easily get annoying.

Close Twitter ticket/Facebook Message one day after status is set to Solved

These are two separate automations, and will be enabled only if the relevant channel (Twitter or Facebook) is also enabled in your instance. The purpose of these automations is to close tickets that are created through these channels more quickly than tickets from other channels. The way that the Twitter and Facebook integrations work is that any incoming correspondence from a customer, regardless of the context, will be added to his latest open ticket in Zendesk. It's possible that the customer might like to start a new conversation and have the details recorded in a new ticket, so this automation proactively assumes that if there is no additional feedback after one day, the ticket should be closed for further updates. Then any future messages from this person on Twitter and Facebook will be created as a new ticket in your Zendesk instance.

Pending notification 24 hours/5 days

These automations are deactivated by default, but I encourage you to enable them. The purpose of these automations is to send customers a reminder email when their tickets are marked as Pending (i.e., the agent is waiting for feedback from the requester). Without these reminders, there's a much smaller chance that the customer will add an update to her ticket. If you enable these automations, it's very important that you review the description of the Pending status (refer back to "Ticket Status" on page 96), and understand that it should be used only to indicate that the ticket is waiting on feedback from the customer, not feedback from someone else at your organization.

Automation Examples

The default Zendesk automations already provide some good examples of processes that can be automated, but here are some more examples that might give you ideas for additional business rules:

Remind agents about unsolved tickets after 48 hours

We use this automation in our own Zendesk instances, and it's an example of what we call a *fortification automation*. It prevents tickets from slipping through the cracks, especially if the ticket has been open for a long time. To configure this automation, set the conditions as shown in Figure 8-9 and the actions as shown in Figure 8-10.

Figure 8-9. Conditions for the "Remind agents about unsolved tickets after 48 hours" automation

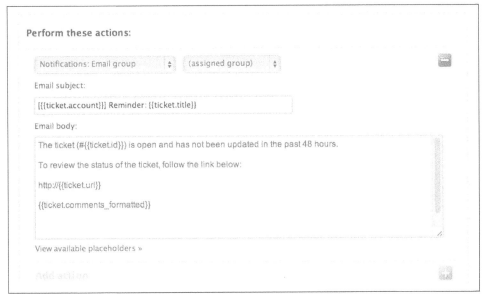

Figure 8-10. Actions for the "Remind agents about unsolved tickets after 48 hours" automation

Escalate unsolved VIP tickets after 72 hours

This automation ties nicely into my example usage of the user and organization tagging feature. If you tag some special users with the "vip" tag, all of the tickets created by those users will be automatically tagged with "vip." Then you can write an automation that checks all tickets with this specific tag, and sets the priority of the ticket to Urgent if it has not been solved within 72 hours. When the automation updates the ticket with the new priority, as a side effect it will also fire the "Notify managers of urgent tickets" trigger from "Trigger Examples" on page 135, which in turn would email the support manager. You can see how these different features start to connect, and hopefully understand the reasons why we call tags the glue that holds the business rules together. To configure this automation, set the conditions as shown in Figure 8-11 and the actions as shown in Figure 8-12.

Automation title

Escalate unsolved VIP tickets after 72 hours

Meet **all** of the following conditions:

| Ticket: Status | Less than | Solved |
| Ticket: Tags | Contains at least one of the following |
| vip |
| Ticket: Hours since created | Is | 72 |

Figure 8-11. Conditions for the "Escalate unsolved VIP tickets after 72 hours" automation

Perform these actions:

| Ticket: Priority | Urgent |

Figure 8-12. Actions for the "Escalate unsolved VIP tickets after 72 hours" automation

Reassign tickets to level 2 support team after one week

After a ticket has been assigned to a support agent for a certain amount of time, it's fairly obvious that the ticket is not being effectively answered by that agent. Often, the agent is the last person to admit it. So you can define an automation that will automatically reassign a ticket to another team if the ticket has not received a response from the current team in an appropriate amount of time. To configure this automation, set the conditions as shown in Figure 8-13 and the actions as shown in Figure 8-14.

Figure 8-13. Conditions for the "Reassign tickets to level 2 support team after one week" automation

Figure 8-14. Actions for the "Reassign tickets to level 2 support team after one week" automation

Nullification of Automations

At some point, every Zendesk administrator will see the following message:

> Automation could not be created as: Automation must contain an action that nullifies a condition. For example, if you have a condition testing for "Priority Is High", you could have an action setting "Priority Is Urgent".

This section is going to explain how to prevent this message from appearing.

But first, let's unpack what this message really means. As mentioned earlier, Zendesk will run your automations once every hour. If you've defined an automation that finds all tickets that have been open for 72 hours or more and changes the status to Urgent, the automation will run as soon as those conditions are met. Let's look at this in more detail:

- 71 hours after the ticket was opened, the conditions *will not* be met, so the automation will not run.

- 72 hours after the ticket was opened, the conditions *will* be met, so the automation will run and the ticket priority will be changed to Urgent.

- 73 hours after the ticket was opened, the conditions *will* be met, so the automation will run and the ticket priority will be changed to Urgent.

- 74 hours after the ticket was opened, the conditions *will* be met, so the automation will run and the ticket priority will be changed to Urgent.

This pattern demonstrates that Zendesk is going to execute a potentially redundant operation on this ticket every hour. The ticket priority was already set to be Urgent at 72 hours, so it's unnecessary to set it again every hour afterward. Zendesk uses a *Multitenant* server architecture, meaning that every Zendesk customer shares the same processing power. Processes that waste power for one customer will also waste the server processing power for every other customer. To avoid this, Zendesk likes to keep things fair and imposes a rule that says that redundant automations should not be repeated on the same ticket.

Fortunately, it's quite easy to add a nullification condition that prevents the automation from running a second time on the same ticket. In the example just shown, this condition would be "Priority is not equal to Urgent." In other words, at 72 hours Zendesk will change the ticket priority, and by having a condition in the automation that checks that the priority has not been changed, at 73 hours the conditions will no longer be met and Zendesk is spared the effort of repeating the automation.

 The general rule to nullifying an automation is that you should write a condition that is the opposite of one of the actions of the automation. If your actions send an email only, the workaround is to add another action that adds a tag to the ticket (e.g., "notification_sent"), then add a condition to the automation to check that the ticket does not have this tag before running the automation again.

Auditing Business Rule Use

If you're on the Plus or Enterprise plans, you can easily identify the triggers and automations that you're actively using, versus the ones that are perhaps no longer needed. To do this, you should open either the triggers or automations administration pages and change the sort order of the rules.

The default sort order for triggers and automations is "Sorted by position," which lists the rules in the order in which they will be executed (see "Ordering Triggers" on page

138 for an explanation of why this is important). The other options for this drop-down list are:

- Sorted by position
- Sorted by creation date, latest first
- Sorted by updated date, latest first
- Sorted by usage over the last hour
- Sorted by usage over the last 24 hours
- Sorted by usage over the last 7 days

If you select one of the options that starts with "Sorted by usage," the most frequently used rules will appear at the top, and you'll get a sense of the value of each of the triggers and automations, based on their usage. If you consistently find that one of the rules is listed as having 0 uses in the past 7 days, it might be that the rule is either improperly configured, or not needed in your Zendesk instance.

 Deactivating these unused rules, while not strictly necessary, will help to reduce the complexity of your Zendesk configuration in the long run, and make it easier to manage Zendesk for other administrators on your team. As a standard practice, we recommend deactivation instead of deletion of business rules, just to maintain the historical context of your Zendesk configuration.

Email Notifications

There is no central page in Zendesk that will allow you to customize the contents of all email notifications that are sent from Zendesk. There is, however, a short list of pages that you can visit to customize the contents, which are listed next. Zendesk gives you a surprising amount of flexibility when it comes to defining the sender address and appearance of your email notifications, which will be explained further in this section.

Bidirectional Email Communication

In "Outgoing Email" on page 21, we explained how to customize the sender email address of your email notifications. In certain situations it might be relevant to enable personalized email replies (covered on page 22). The combination of options selected in your Zendesk instance will have an impact on the way that email notifications are sent to users, and the specific sender address selected for every outgoing email.

When sending email notifications, Zendesk will always use the *primary* email address of the user as the recipient address. Every Zendesk user can have several email addresses on her profile, but only one primary email address. If a user lists only one email address, it will automatically be selected as the primary address. If the user lists multiple addresses on her profile, the primary address must have been previously verified on the user's account.

The sender address of all email notifications will be determined by the options selected on the Email channel administration page. Zendesk uses the *reply-to* address system in emails, which basically means that when a customer clicks Reply, his email will go to an address that's different from the sender of the email. Zendesk automatically generates extra information in the Reply-to email address to help your organization manage information.

For instance, assume that email notification about a ticket comes from *support@blueskies.zendesk.com* or, if personalized email replies are enabled, Erin (Blue Skies Support) *<support@blueskies.zendesk.com>*. The Reply-to address on that email notification would be *support+id123@blueskies.zendesk.com*. Although the sender of the email is *support@blueskies.zendesk.com*, when the user clicks the Reply button in his email tool, the email is automatically sent to *support+id123@blueskies.zendesk.com*. When Zendesk receives this email from the end user, it will add the email contents as a new comment on the ticket with ID 123. You may have noticed that the ticket ID of 123 was subtly included in the Reply-to address in this example.

Similarly, when an email notification is sent to an agent from Zendesk, the sender address uses a unique code instead of the ticket ID, an example being *support+idP6WQ-X8B9@blueskies.zendesk.com*. When an agent replies with an email to this address, the contents of the email will be added as a new comment to the same ticket, although it's impossible to determine the ticket ID from the email address alone. The reason that a unique code is added for agents but the plain ticket ID is used for end users is to add a layer of security to agent emails. It's possible to spoof an email address (meaning that you could send an email and pretend to be sending it from an address that is not yours), so it's theoretically possible for an end user to maliciously pretend to be an agent by sending an email into Zendesk from a spoofed agent's address. This will add her email as an agent comment to the ticket. To prevent this from happening, Zendesk generates a unique code (in our example, "P6WQ-X8B9") for each agent/ticket combination. Even if the malicious user was able to spoof the sender address, it's probabilistically impossible for her to guess the correct code, which adds a layer of security to the process and ensures that only agents are able to add private notes to restricted tickets via email.

To ensure that replies to email notifications go to the correct place, your agents and end users should not change the recipient email address when replying to email notifications from Zendesk. Regardless of the contents of the email, if a response is sent to the standard *support@blueskies.zendesk.com* email address in this situation, it would be created as a new ticket instead of being added as a comment on the existing ticket.

Email Notification Template

The source code for the outgoing email template—in HTML format—can be found in the Email section of the Channels administration page, and is also provided here. The default template is set up to be clean and simple and to contain the most relevant information. The template deliberately does not use any branding or colors, meaning that you don't have to be concerned that the colors will conflict with your corporate color scheme. There are also no logos or custom fonts used in the email template. If you want to do all of these things and you have a basic understanding of HTML, you can modify the template yourself by finding the text area labeled "HTML template" on the Email administration page.

```
<!DOCTYPE html PUBLIC "-//W3C//DTD XHTML 1.0 Transitional//EN"
  "http://www.w3.org/TR/xhtml1/DTD/xhtml1-transitional.dtd">
<html>
<head>
  <meta http-equiv="Content-Type" content="text/html; charset=utf-8" />
  <style type="text/css">
    table td {
      border-collapse: collapse;
    }
  </style>
</head>
<body style="width: 100%!important; margin: 0; padding: 0;">
  <div style="padding: 10px ; line-height: 18px;
    font-family: 'Lucida Grande',Verdana,Arial,sans-serif;
    font-size: 12px; color:#444444;">
    <div style="color: #b5b5b5;">{{delimiter}}</div>
    {{content}}
    <div style="color: #aaaaaa; margin: 10px 0 14px 0; padding-top: 10px;
      border-top: 1px solid #eeeeee;">
      {{footer}}.  Delivered by <a href="http://www.zendesk.com"
      style="color:black" target="_new">Zendesk</a>.
    </div>
  </div>
</body>
</html>
```

We generally don't recommend that administrators change the email template in Zendesk. Email notifications from Zendesk aren't a marketing opportunity or a branding exercise. They are a simple piece of communication that is sent to customers. It's generally unnecessary to incorporate a flashy look and feel into something as simple as an email notification.

After you've settled on the template of your email notifications, the contents of your emails can be found on any of the following pages:

Customers
> New users to Zendesk will receive emails with text that is defined on this administration page.

Tickets
> The message offered to CC'ed users can be customized on this administration page.

Triggers
> Described in more details in "Triggers" on page 132, these are the email notifications sent to users when a ticket is updated. You'll need to open each of the triggers and read the actions to customize the contents of the emails.

Automations
> Described in "Automations" on page 140, these email notifications will be sent to users based on the time criteria determined by administrators. Just like triggers, you'll need to open up each of the automations to adjust the contents.

Mail Delimiter

Below the email template on the Email channel administration page is an option named "Mail delimiter." The default value for this field is `{{txt.email.delimiter}}`, which is a system placeholder that references the following message, translated if necessary into the language you use:

> *## Please do not write below this line ##*

In the email notifications sent from Zendesk, the mail delimiter text will be placed above the part of the email generated by Zendesk, but below the section where the recipient would enter his comment when replying to the email. When Zendesk receives the email response from the user, it will exclude everything below the line because it believes it to have been generated from Zendesk itself, and keeps only the content above. There's a slight risk that the sender of the email will have used inline editing, which means that he added his specific comments further down the email response. To avoid this, the mail delimiter message tries to be very specific about the importance of not writing below the line.

We've never really found a compelling reason to change the value of the mail delimiter. Zendesk does a good job of stating a simple message to the user, and translates the message into all available languages in the product. It's possible that you'd want to write your own message because the default one does not suit your purposes, but that's very rare.

Placeholders

When your agents define the text of macros or when you define the text in email notifications as an administrator, this text must be dynamic to be useful in a broad range of circumstances. For example, your email notifications may contain some instructions that refer specifically to the status or priority of a ticket. *Placeholders* will allow you to dynamically include specific field values in your comments.

There are several options to find the complete list of Zendesk placeholders:

- When you select the "Comment/description" option in a macro, beneath the text area there is a link labeled "View available placeholders." Clicking this link will expand the page to list the set of available placeholders.

- If you select the option to "Email user" or "Email group" from a trigger or automation, the same link will appear beneath the text area on this page.

- Zendesk has documented the complete set of placeholders (*http://bit.ly/zen-desk-ref*) in its knowledge base.

Before you build shared macros for your team or write your trigger and automation emails, it's worth investing some time into understanding placeholders and their role in the product.

Customer Satisfaction

For most support managers, the metric that is most important for customer service is the current size of the ticket backlog. The backlog is the major factor that will influence response times, and potentially the quality of the responses from your support team. While the response times and number of tickets answered are useful metrics, the fact is that they do not accurately reflect the level of *satisfaction* experienced by customers seeking support from your organization. Fortunately, Zendesk has a feature named *Customer Satisfaction* that serves this purpose, and it is available to customers on the Regular, Plus, and Enterprise plans.

Zendesk's customer satisfaction feature is unique because, like most of the product, Zendesk has deliberately made the feature simple. The question asked to customers is:

> *How would you rate the support you received?*

The options for the response are either "Good, I'm satisfied," or "Bad, I'm unsatisfied." It's not possible to change the question, and it's not possible to change the options for the response. By deliberately keeping this question simple and avoiding a scale of 1–10 like many other systems have, Zendesk has successfully increased the response rate in its customer satisfaction surveys to well above the industry standard. As a comparison, the industry average response rate for customer satisfaction surveys is below 10%, and the response rates on Zendesk's survey range from 18% to 25% (depending on the geographic region).

To enable this feature, you'll need to open the Satisfaction tab on the Customers administration page and select the checkbox labeled "Allow customers to rate tickets." As described in "Automations" on page 140, this will immediately create a new automation that emails customers 24 hours after their ticket is solved to ask for feedback on their support experience.

 If you've enabled this feature, it might also be worth revisiting the shared views (covered on page 123) that you've defined and adding the Satisfaction column to any views that include solved or closed tickets. This is an easy way to view the customer satisfaction of many tickets at the same time.

CHAPTER 9

Help Center

In a way, Zendesk is really two products in one. The first product is the ticketing system, which includes most of the features that we've described up until this point in the book. The other product is the *Help Center*, a self-service portal where your customers can find answers to their questions without engaging with your support team directly.

In his book *High-Tech, High-Touch Customer Service*, Micah Solomon describes the growth of self-service portals (similar to Zendesk's Help Center) with the observation, "self-service[…] is a powerful trend in customer service, and companies that ignore it, pursue it reluctantly, or violate the basic laws of its implementation will be left in the dust." To companies who are not observing this trend, "customer service" is delivered through a person-to-person interaction, and anything else seems impersonal or robotic. But really, customers are becoming more satisfied when companies are able to anticipate their needs, and provide the answers to their questions immediately, without human intervention.

Within the Help Center there are two distinct but closely tied features—the knowledge base and community. Only administrators and agents can manage the knowledge base and contribute articles to it. Your end users are the consumers of the content in your knowledge base. This is where you'll publish FAQs, user manuals, and any other content that will help customers find their own answers to any number of questions and support issues they may encounter.

The other half of the Help Center is community, which is where your customers can post questions and ideas that can be responded to either by agents or other members of your user community. It's designed around a simple question-and-answer model, and users can vote answers up or down. Every question or idea can have an official answer that is shown just below the question so that it's easily visible to users.

In addition to the knowledge base and community, your Help Center is where your users sign up and create an account in your Zendesk instance, submit support requests, chat with agents, and track their tickets. It provides every tool you need to enable your users to help themselves and, when that's not enough, to interact with your agents.

Terms and Definitions

Before getting started with the Help Center, I'll provide a quick introduction to the terms that are specific to Zendesk's self-service portal, starting with the knowledge base:

Category

As your knowledge base grows and you start to add more information, a logical structure becomes important. Categories are useful for this purpose and provide visual order to the knowledge base. Otherwise, it may seem disorganized. A sample category from the Zendesk knowledge base is "Product news and updates," which is also visible in Figure 9-1. A category may contain multiple sections.

Section

Categories contain sections, and sections contain articles. Sections are used to refer to a collection of articles on a specific subject area. Just like categories, sections help to collect your information together in a logical way. Otherwise, your articles would be unstructured and hard for your readers to find. An example section from Zendesk's "Product news and updates" category is Announcements.

Article

An article typically contains information on only one subject. For example, a sample article from the Zendesk knowledge base is "Introducing an all new email notification template." Each article can be associated with one section.

The use of these concepts is demonstrated in Figure 9-1, which shows a category of "Product news and updates," a section called Announcements, and an article called "Introducing an all new email notification template."

In the community, content is organized in the following ways:

Topic

You can think of these as discussion topics, an area in the community where users post questions and ideas about a specific topic. For example, there might be topics for each of your products, or distinct features within a product, or something more generalized like a "Best practices" or "Tips" topic. End users can add questions and ideas to existing topics.

Question

This is the essence of community in Zendesk. The question model works extremely well as a way for customers to publicly request help for an issue they have. As answered questions begin to accumulate in your community, by extension your knowledge base is growing as well. In most cases, a question asked by one user will at some point be asked by other users. By searching your Help Center for keywords contained within the question, or navigating through topics, users will locate the original question and see the answers provided.

Idea

This is a way for your user community to share ideas with other members of the community or with your business. For example, you might be open to hearing how your customers would like to see your product grow and improve and posting an idea allows them to do that. Ideas may also be tips that users share with other users in your community. We've described question and idea separately here, but they are actually a single action in the community. When your users want to contribute either, they click the "Post a question or idea" button.

Answer

Answers are the conversation around a question. Many questions may not have one clear and absolute answer, and your users will weigh in with their own ideas and experiences. Evaluating the quality of answers and deciding which is the definitive answer (if possible) is the result of either feedback from the community or intervention from an agent who's marked one of the answers as the official answer. When that happens, the answer is moved to the top of the list of answers and is clearly visible below the original question.

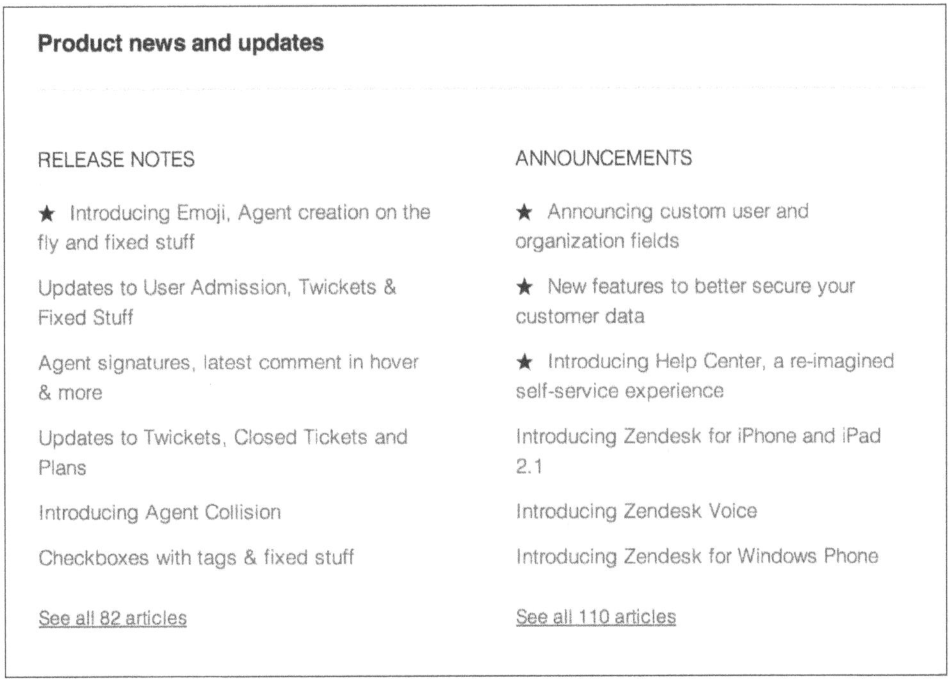

Product news and updates

RELEASE NOTES

★ Introducing Emoji, Agent creation on the fly and fixed stuff

Updates to User Admission, Twickets & Fixed Stuff

Agent signatures, latest comment in hover & more

Updates to Twickets, Closed Tickets and Plans

Introducing Agent Collision

Checkboxes with tags & fixed stuff

See all 82 articles

ANNOUNCEMENTS

★ Announcing custom user and organization fields

★ New features to better secure your customer data

★ Introducing Help Center, a re-imagined self-service experience

Introducing Zendesk for iPhone and iPad 2.1

Introducing Zendesk Voice

Introducing Zendesk for Windows Phone

See all 110 articles

Figure 9-1. Examples of the knowledge base hierarchy

Help Center Users

There are several different types of users with varying permissions in the Help Center. These include the following:

Help Center Manager
> By default, all Zendesk administrators are Help Center Managers. This role can also be extended to agents. As the name implies, administrators and agents with this role are responsible for managing the Help Center. This means customizing it, configuring access options, and setting the structure of the knowledge base and community by creating categories and sections and predefined community topics.

Agents
> Agents that are not granted the Help Center Manager role can view all public content and areas of the Help Center that are restricted to agents only. Agents can add articles in the sections of the knowledge base that they have access to.

End Users
> An end user is somebody who has signed into the Help Center and who is not an agent or administrator. End users in Zendesk can access the public knowledge base and the public community. They can add comments to knowledge base articles but cannot add articles to it. If an end user wants to contribute, he can do so by posting a new question or idea in the community and providing answers to existing questions and ideas. End users can also follow knowledge base sections and articles, follow topics and questions and ideas in the community, submit support requests, and track their existing requests.

Anonymous users
> These are end users who have not signed into your Help Center. These users can read articles that are open for public access, but cannot add comments to those articles or contribute questions or answers to the community unless they sign in. Zendesk does not allow anonymous user contributions to the Help Center, which is done to help prevent spam. If you allow anyone to submit tickets, these users will see and can use the support request form. They will not, however, be able to track those requests unless they create an account in your Zendesk instance and then sign into your Help Center.

Configuring the Help Center

The Help Center is a separate application from the administrator and agent application. The two "speak" to each other, but they exist in separate web browser windows. Most of the Help Center configuration is done in the Help Center application, but there are several settings in the Customers administration page that affect the Help Center and which I describe in "Customer Administration Settings" on page 158. You'll find the link to the Help Center in the sidebar. It's the life preserver icon. When you click that icon, the Help Center will open in a new browser window, as shown in Figure 9-2, and you'll see a menu in the lower-right corner of the screen. This is where you manage content, customize the Help Center, and configure general settings.

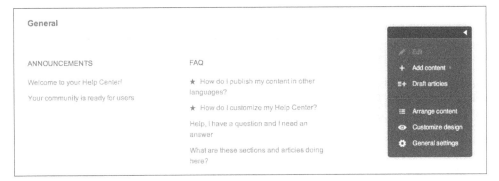

Figure 9-2. The Help Center menu

 Your Help Center isn't live to the public until you activate it. You'll see a message at the top of the Help Center prompting you to do so (it's also available in General Settings). Our recommendation is to activate your Help Center only when it's configured, customized, and ready to be used by your customers. As you're branding it, adding content, and configuring features, it'll be a work in progress and you may go through many iterations of the design and layout. Save the activation until that work is done. Once it's activated, it cannot be deactivated unless you contact the Zendesk Support team.

On the General Settings page, you can set the following options for your Help Center:

Communities
This setting toggles the community feature in the Help Center on or off. It's selected on by default.

Mobile layout
This setting enables a mobile-friendly layout for users who access your Help Center using smartphones and tablets. The layout will be optimized for those formats and much easier to use and read. If this isn't enabled, your users will see the standard layout that is designed to be viewed on a desktop web browser. You'll also be able to set a few simple branding options for the mobile layout. By necessity, the mobile layout cannot be as highly customized as the desktop layout.

Google Analytics

If you want to use Google Analytics to track the activity in your Help Center, and you should, you can enter your Google Tracking ID here. This, of course, is something you need to acquire outside of your Help Center by creating a Google Analytics account. After you enable this setting and enter your tracking ID, you can track not only the number of page views and many other metrics that Google Analytics offers, but also search events. These include the number of times users submit a search per minute and the search terms used. Search terms with no results will help you determine where you've got gaps in your knowledge base.

Display unsafe content

With Zendesk's focus on security, this setting is here to help prevent malicious code from being added to the HTML content that is inserted into your Help Center. When this setting is enabled, the HTML tags that are considered unsafe are not actually stripped from the content; they're just not included in the HTTP responses sent to browsers when your users click an article. The Zendesk knowledge base article on this subject (*http://bit.ly/zen-help*) lists the HTML tags and attributes that are considered safe.

Require sign-in

If you want a "restricted" Help Center, meaning that only registered users can see the content and use your Help Center, you need to enable this setting. Unregistered and logged-out users see only the sign-up and password reset pages.

Languages and name

This is where you can translate the name of your Help Center into the other languages that you support. These are the languages you chose on the Localization tab of the Account administration page. Each language you enabled is displayed here, and you can enter the translated version of the name of your Help Center.

After you've finished updating the settings on this page, click the Save button; your settings will be immediately enabled.

Customer Administration Settings

As mentioned earlier, most of the Help Center configuration is done in the Help Center itself. Here are the exceptions, which are settings on the Customers administration page:

Your Zendesk account name

This is name that is displayed on the sign-in page.

Require CAPTCHA

When this setting is selected, a CAPTCHA prompt will be added to the support request form in your Help Center. This requires users to type in the words that are displayed as graphics and ensures that the support request is being made by a human rather than a computer program, which helps to prevent spam.

Ask users to register

This setting, which won't be visible to you until after you've activated your Help Center, requires your users to create an account in your Help Center and then to verify their email address and create a password. Until they've done that, their support requests are held in limbo and are not added to your Zendesk ticket queue.

Allow users to view and edit their profile data

This setting allows users to edit their own user profile in the Help Center by adding the "Edit my profile" link to the user menu in the upper-right corner. Users can change their name, add an avatar, enter their phone number, and select their time zone.

Allow users to change their password

This setting allows users to change their own passwords by adding the "Change password" link to the user menu.

Adding Categories and Sections

As an administrator, you are also a Help Center Manager and have complete control over the Help Center. If you'd like to delegate this responsibility to another member of your team without giving them full administrative privileges to your Zendesk instance, you can assign an agent to the Help Center Manager role by editing her profile and selecting the Manager option in the Help Center field. If you're on the Enterprise plan, you can grant this permission to an agent role by selecting the "Can manage Help Center" option. See "Enterprise Agent Roles and Light Agents" on page 42 for details on how to do this.

New Help Center instances do not appear to contain any knowledge base categories, although you'll see a number of sections containing some example articles. When you create your first category, all of those example sections will be placed into a category called General, which is a hidden cateogry and not displayed until you create your own first category. You can, and most likely will, delete this category and its example sections before you activate your Help Center. You can also just set each section's view setting to "Only agents," and those sections and the General category that they are contained in will not be shown to end users. To add a new category, click "Add content" in the Help Center menu and then select Category from the list. When you add a category, there are really no parameters for you to specify except the name of the category and a description. After you've entered these values, submit the form by clicking Add, and your category will be created.

After you add categories, the next step is to start adding sections to the category. To do this, you again click "Add content" (see Figure 9-3) and then select Section. As with categories, you add a section name and an optional description. You place sections into categories by selecting a category from the "Show in category" drop-down list. You can also order the articles in a section manually, by the creation date, and alphabetically. The section access settings are described in "Section Access Restrictions" on page 161.

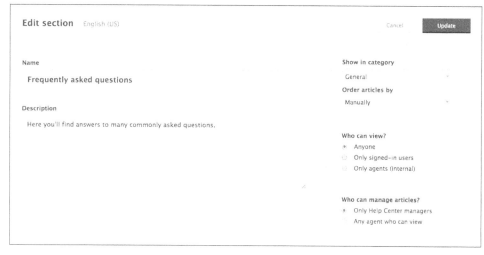

Figure 9-3. Examples of the knowledge base hierarchy

Arranging Categories, Sections, and Articles

You can arrange the order of your categories, sections, and articles by clicking "Arrange content" in the Help Center menu (see Figure 9-4). This page displays all of these elements in a hierarchical list. To rearrange any of these elements, you simply drag and drop them to a new location.

Figure 9-4. The drag-and-drop interface to arrange categories, sections, and articles

After you've finished rearranging your content, click the Update button to save your new knowledge base content order.

Section Access Restrictions

Even though the knowledge base is meant for public access, you might want to restrict some of your sections to be visible only to certain people. One example would be an agent-only section, which has answers to common questions as a reference point for your support agents. Another example might be a special section dedicated to customers on your platinum support package, or customers who are running a beta of your software product. Using the tools described in this section, you are able to restrict section access based on such criteria. All of the following options can be found on the page to create or edit a section:

Who can view?
> It's possible to restrict the articles in this section to be visible to anyone (meaning anonymous users who are not signed into your Help Center), only to users who are signed in, signed-in users from a specific organizations or who have specific tags in their user profile, or agents only. If you select the agents-only option, you can further restrict access by groups or tags. If you elect to leave the section visible to anyone, the articles will also be indexed by search engines such as Google, and will be returned in search results that contain the keywords in the articles. Most customers like this feature, and we refer to it in "Referring Macros to the Knowledge Base" on page 128 as a specific benefit of using the knowledge base to publish answers to common questions.

Who can manage articles?
> This setting is relevant only to internal users, your Help Center Managers and agents. End users can only read and add comments to knowledge base articles. The two options are "Only Help Center Managers" and "Any agent who can view." The first is straightforward; if you're a Help Center Manager, you can manage these articles. The second option means any agents in your Zendesk instance unless the section has been restricted to a specific group or groups or tags. For agents, *manage* means the ability to add and then edit the articles in the sections they are allowed to view. Agents can manage any articles in the section, including articles created by other agents. By the way, agents include Light Agents in the Enterprise plan.

It's possible to combine public and private sections in the same category, but you can't do that with articles in a section. The section view setting determines if all the articles are public or private. This is not set at the article level.

Multilanguage Knowledge Base

If you're on the Plus or Enterprise plans, it's possible to enable other languages in your Help Center. All of the additional languages you chose to add in the Localization tab of the Account administration page, described in "Multilanguage Support for End Users" on page 16, are supported in the Help Center. Enabling those languages does two things. The first is that the Help Center automatically provides a translated user interface for each language, and users can choose from those languages by selecting one from the language selector (see Figure 9-5) that appears at the top of the Help Center, next to the user menu.

Figure 9-5. The Help Center language selector

Second, as shown in Figure 9-6, those languages are added to the content elements within the knowledge base: Category, Section, and Article. When editing any of those elements, you'll see that you can create a language-specific version for each.

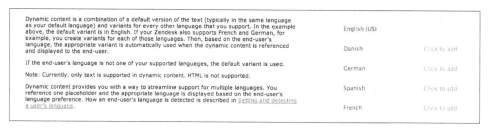

Figure 9-6. Adding translated versions of categories, sections, and articles

Your default language determines which language is shown by default, and this means the translations of the words in the user interface and the content elements in the knowledge base. The default language in our Zendesk is English, and when we add any one of the content elements in the knowledge base, this is the default. If we add a new article, it's flagged as "English (US)." If no other language has been selected, this is the language our users will see. This is also the language of the content provided in our knowledge base if no other translated versions of the content were provided.

If you want to provide translations in other languages (e.g., an article), click to add a new language version, and you'll be able to add translated text to that version. When a user selects that language, the translated version of the article is shown. But there's a caveat here. For an article to display in another language, the section and category that the article is contained within must also have a translated version.

It's not possible to show more than one language at a time in the Help Center. After you create translated versions of your knowledge base content, that is the only content that is displayed. For example, if you translate just one section of your knowledge base into Portuguese, your Portuguese users will see only that section, not all the other English language content available in your knowledge base. They'd have to switch to English to see that content.

As you're creating translated versions of your articles, you can mark them as hidden if they are not ready to be published. Edit the translated version of the article and click the Hidden checkbox that is located above the article's title.

Draft Articles

One of our favorite features in the Help Center is the ability to develop new knowledge base content and mark that content as draft until it's ready to be published. This allows your content developers to work directly in your knowledge base and create draft articles without having to otherwise create a restricted section or sections and place all the articles there. You do need to select the category and section that the article will eventually be published to, but that's just an article setting, not its physical location while in draft mode.

To create a draft article, click "Draft articles" in the Help Center menu and then select "Add draft." The article editor is opened and you can compose the article. Translated versions of draft articles can also be created. As you create draft articles, you see them listed on the Draft Articles page along with the date each was created and updated. You click a draft article's title to edit it. When you're ready to publish the article, edit the article, deselect the "Draft mode" setting, and save the article by clicking the Update button. Your article is immediately published into the category and section you chose when creating the article. Help Center Managers can see and edit all draft articles. Agents can see and edit the draft articles in the sections they have access to. You can also move any existing published articles into draft mode by selecting the "Draft mode" setting.

Community

As explained in "Terms and Definitions" on page 154, the community part of your Help Center is where your users can post questions and ideas and provide answers and comments to those posts. Communities are organized around topics, and questions and ideas are added to those topics. The community sits alongside your knowledge base, and you can access it by clicking the "community browse" link. There isn't actually much to configure in your community other than to seed it with topics.

Figure 9-7 demonstrates how you can look at the community in three different ways. First you'll see the Topics view; this is similar to the knowledge base in that content is organized into containers. In the knowledge base, it's categories and sections; in the community, it's topics. Their purpose is to gather questions and ideas together into thematically related groupings. You might, for example, have a topic for each product and service you provide. You can set up your community with these topics and your users can add more as they see fit. Users can view either all the topics or just those that they have chosen to follow.

Figure 9-7. Community navigation in the Help Center

You can also view your community by questions and ideas—meaning that you can view them in a list without their being contained within topics. Click Questions at the top of the page, and you'll see the list of questions. You can filter this list by Newest, Recommended, Trending, Votes, and Following. We'll cover these in a little more detail later in this chapter.

The third view of your community is Unanswered. These are the questions and ideas that either have no official answer or no upvoted answers. You can also view the questions and ideas that have received no answers.

Questions and Ideas

Everything in the community is built around the question. The button to create a new question says "Questions and Ideas," but *Ideas* is really only there to extend the use of a question to include ideas; that is, not just "hey, I've got a question" but also "hey, I've got this great idea to share." Either intention, asking a question or sharing an idea, is handled by the same form. You enter a title and description and then select the topic you want it added to. Questions/ideas can be plain text or Markdown. Using Markdown, you can insert URL references to images and attachments. Zendesk provides a knowledge base article (*https://support.zendesk.com/entries/21714462*) that describes how to use Markdown formatting.

After a question/idea has been posted, the person who posted it expects a response from someone. Just because this is the community part of your Help Center, don't expect that someone from your user community will respond to the question/idea, let alone in a timely manner. It takes some effort and time to build an active user community. We strongly recommend that you assign one or more agents to monitor your Help Center and ensure that questions are responded to as quickly as possible. This includes the community questions as well as comments posted in your knowledge base. Activity will breed more activity. Users will quickly drop this support channel if there is little or no activity and instead resort to opening tickets and relying on your agents to provide them with the answers they need. A healthy self-service channel is one of the best ways to deflect tickets and take the load off of your agents. An easy way to monitor activity is to watch the list of unanswered questions.

Help Center Customization

Customization as it's used here means customizing the design of the Help Center, and Zendesk has made this very easy to do. The layout is based on themes, which is similar to how popular blog and website building applications handle customization. If you've ever created a blog using any of the popular blogging applications—such as WordPress, Blogger, or Squarespace—you'll quickly see that the customization tools that Zendesk provides are very similar.

You access all the customization tools from the "Customize design" link (as shown in Figure 9-8) in the Help Center menu. This opens the design editor on the lefthand side of your browser. There are four main sections in the editor: Themes, Appearance, Branding, and Mobile Branding. In each of these sections, you'll see the design settings that affect your Help Center.

Figure 9-8. The customization tools in Help Center

Themes and Simple Design Changes

The Help Center comes with five standard themes that you can use as is or use as the basis of a custom theme. Each has a different visual layout. You can choose from any of these five playfully named themes: The Wiry Merchant, The Curious Wind, The Noble Feast, The Humble Squid, and The Swiftest Elk. The differences between them are mostly visual; each one displays most of the default elements of the Help Center, as you can see by selecting different themes in the editor. The Wiry Merchant theme emphasizes the search box and places this as the dominant visual element on the home page. The Humble Squid emphasizes the knowledge base categories and presents those as boxes in rows and columns, which can quickly help steer users to specific products or services, if that's important to you. The default color palette for each theme is subdued, using mostly white, black, blue, and gray—ready for you to brand them with your own palette of colors.

Figure 9-9 illustrates how you can make simple color and font changes using the Appearance panel in the design editor. If you want to change the background of the search box in The Wiry Merchant theme, just reset Color 1 using a hex number or the color picker. As you change each color, you'll see where they are used in the design. This panel is where you can also change the fonts that are used.

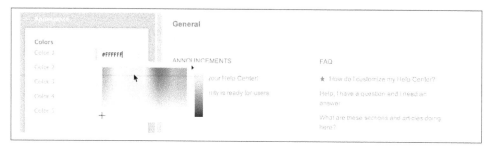

Figure 9-9. Setting colors using the color picker

In the Branding panel, you can set the name of your Help Center, add your logo to the header, and add a favicon (the graphic shown in the address bar in a browser). You might be wondering why the Help Center name is in two places (here and on the General Settings page). The explanation is simple: it's in both these places for your convenience. If you change the name in the Branding section, it will also be changed on the General Settings page, and vice versa. However, the translated names for your Help Center can be set only on the General Settings page.

Finally, if you selected the Mobile layout option on the General Settings page, the Mobile Branding panel will also be available. Your customization options for the mobile layout are restricted to changing the logo and selecting the color that is displayed in the header.

With the design editor open, you can quickly preview how your Help Center will look to each type of user: Help Center Manager, agent, end user, and anonymous. In the lower-right corner of the screen, you'll see the "Previewing As" tool where you can select a user type. While the visual design is the same for all users, content may not be, and this tool shows you what content can be seen by each of these users. This is a great way to check that all of your internal content has been restricted and is indeed being hidden from end users.

Advanced Customization

You can use any of the themes as is or you can use one as the basis for a more elaborate customization. Many of Zendesk's customers take advantage of this and create Help Center designs that radically depart from the base theme. A great example of this is the Rockstar Games Help Center (*http://support.rockstargames.com*). It's designed its Help Center to match the design of its website. You can do the same thing if you're comfortable with CSS (Cascading Style Sheets) and, optionally, JavaScript. But before we explain that, it's important to understand what the building blocks of a Help Center theme are.

With the design editor open, you'll see the "Edit theme" link in the Theme panel (see Figure 9-10). Click that link and you'll see the code editor. There are four views in the editor: HTML, CSS, JS, and Assets.

The first thing you might notice is how simple the HTML structure is. This is because themes are built from predefined components. These are the placeholders shown in the editor (e.g., `{{category_tree}}`). Each of the elements on the page is displayed in the theme using these component placeholders. If you click the arrow next to "HTML: Home page," you'll see that each page in the theme and the header and footer are selectable and can be edited separately. You can rearrange the components on the page or delete and add components as needed. To see all the components that can be used on each HTML page, you click the "View available components" link below the code editor.

You use the CSS and JS code editors to modify the underlying code. The CSS editor gives you fine-grained control of your Help Center design, and the JS editor allows you to modify the page behavior and change the titles of some key elements on the page. For example, you could use JavaScript to insert a custom menu into the header or footer, which is something many Zendesk customers have done. If you're not familiar or are not comfortable with these tools, you can make someone else (e.g., a web designer) a Help Center Manager so that she can do this work. Customization at this level is beyond the scope of this book, but Zendesk provides an excellent CSS cookbook (*http://bit.ly/css-ckbk*) that contains many CSS examples for commonly modified elements in a theme. These include modifications such as changing the background color of the header and footer and changing the appearance of article links and titles. A detailed component reference (*http://bit.ly/comp-ref*) is also available in the Zendesk knowledge base.

```
Theme editor — The Swiftest Elk

HTML: Home page  ▾      CSS  │  JS  │  Assets                          (⟩ Preview

 1 ▾ <section class="hero-unit">
 2       {{search_bar}}
 3   </section>
 4
 5 ▾ <section class="clearfix">
 6 ▾    <div class="knowledge-base">
 7         {{category_tree}}
 8       </div>
 9 ▾    <div class="community">
10         {{community_header}}
11         {{trending_questions}}
12         {{community_header.internal}}
13         {{trending_questions.internal}}
14       </div>
15   </section>
16

View available components
```

Figure 9-10. The HTML structure in the code editor

 When you're in the code editor, you can search the code by clicking Ctrl+F (in Windows) or Cmd+F (on OS X). When you do this, a search tool appears in the editor, which you can use to quickly locate elements in the code.

Promoted Articles

To illustrate how easy it is to use components, this example explains how to place important articles on the home page of your theme. Figure 9-11 demonstrates how to designate and highlight an article in your knowledge base as being important in order to promote it. You do that by editing the article and selecting the Promoted option. You'll see that all promoted articles are starred and placed at the top of the section in which they are contained.

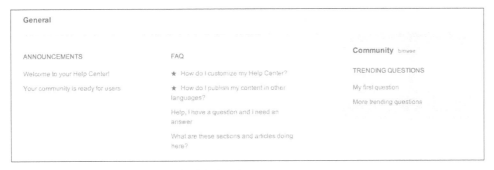

Figure 9-11. Promoted articles highlighted in a section

To get those promoted articles into one list and place it on the home page, you use the `{{promoted_articles}}` component. You start by clicking "Customize design" in the Help Center menu, then editing your theme by clicking "Edit theme." For example, suppose that you're using The Swiftest Elk theme and you want to place the promoted articles just below the search box, as shown in Figure 9-12. To do that, you insert a new line below the `{{search_bar}}` component and add the `{{promoted_articles}}` component.

```
Theme editor - Custom Theme 2

HTML: Home page  ▾  |  CSS  |  JS  |  Assets                    ⟨⟩ Preview

1 ▾ <section class="hero-unit">
2       {{search_bar}}
3       {{promoted_articles}}
4   </section>
5
6 ▾ <section class="clearfix">
7 ▾   <div class="knowledge-base">
8         {{category_tree}}
9     </div>
```

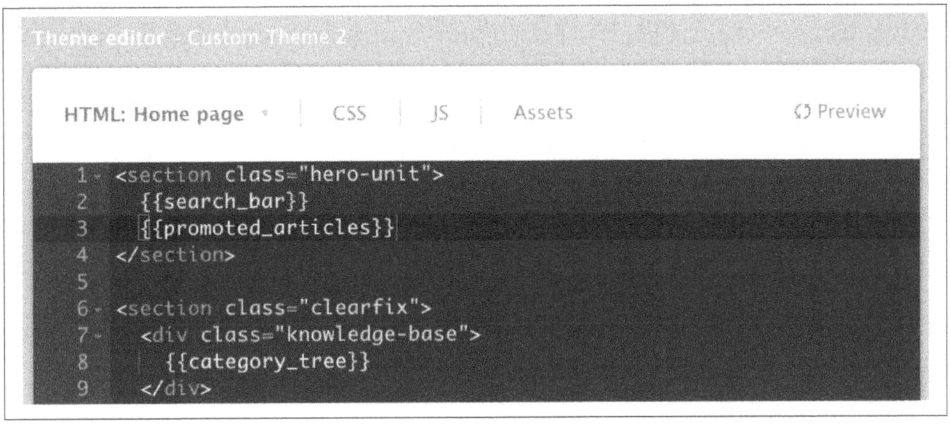

Figure 9-12. Adding the promoted articles component to the home page

You can preview what that looks like by clicking Preview, or you can just save the theme changes by clicking Save and then Publish Changes. Figure 9-13 shows how the promoted articles display on the home page.

Figure 9-13. The promoted articles list on the home page

Google Analytics

As you're populating your knowledge base with useful articles, it's important to measure the value that is being delivered to your customers, and the ways in which you can increase this value. Using Google Analytics with your Help Center provides the sort of analysis that will help you to make these decisions.

After you've configured Google Analytics in your Help Center (described in "Configuring the Help Center" on page 156), every search that your users perform will be logged, along with the results of the search, and the specific search terms used. To find this information, you can use the Site Search tools, which are included in the Behavior section of Google Analytics.

The details of working with Google Analytics are outside the scope of this book, but I wanted to point out one tool in Google Analytics that will help you determine what your Help Center users are searching for and what your most popular articles are.

> The Zendesk knowledge base contains a series of four articles (*http://bit.ly/zen_google*) that dive deep into best practices for using Google Analytics with your Help Center, and they're highly recommended.

Ensure relevance of top results
The Search Terms page lists the search terms that your customers have used to find information in your knowledge base. Each search term is also linked to a list of articles that were returned in the search. If you click the search term in the left column, you'll have access to that list of results. Your goal here is to ensure that the most relevant article appears at the top of the list because most users assume that's the first result they're going to see. If the article you want to see at the top of the list isn't, you can modify the title to include the search term that was used and also add the search term to the body of the article if you haven't already done so.

Check the accuracy of top results

Top results are the most important ones in your Zendesk knowledge base, because they get the most visitors. It's a good idea to regularly review the list of top results from the Search Terms page, and update the contents of these topics if they are out of date. Not all of your articles will be 100% accurate all of the time, but using the Search Terms page helps to at least ensure that the most popular results are subject to an active review process.

These are just a few of the things you can do to monitor and constantly improve the information in your knowledge base. As your number of tickets increases, you'll also have more material to contribute back to your knowledge base; and after a little while, your Help Center will be so populated with information that the process of providing support to your customers will be so simple that it's *almost zen-like*.

About the Authors

Stafford Vaughan started computer programming at an early age. He grew up near Sydney, Australia, before moving to Silicon Valley to join Apple as a Training Program Manager. He has spent the majority of his career building training departments for fast-growing software companies and personally established the Zendesk public training program in 2011.

As an educator, Stafford has authored the official training curricula for Zendesk, Atlassian JIRA, Confluence, GreenHopper, and GoodData. He has delivered training sessions to more than 1,000 organizations in 15 countries, including NASA, the Pentagon, the United Nations in Geneva, Harvard University, Stanford Graduate School of Business, Groupon, the US Department of Commerce, Sun Microsystems, and Wells Fargo Bank.

Stafford holds a bachelor of software engineering degree from the University of Newcastle, and he is a CompTIA Certified Technical Trainer, a Sun Certified Java Programmer, a Microsoft Certified Application Specialist, an Apple Certified Pro, and an Adobe Certified Expert.

Stafford currently lives in San Francisco, and in his spare time he enjoys photography, hiking, and relaxing with his partner, Kenny.

Anton de Young is the Director of Customer Education and Community at Zendesk, where he manages the team that creates all of the user-guide documentation and all of the training available to Zendesk customers. His team also manages the community of users who contribute so much to the Zendesk support portal (*http:// www.support.zendesk.com*).

When Anton joined Zendesk in 2011, he was the only writer, and after creating the first version of the Zendesk user guide himself, he began building a team of writers, instructional designers, and trainers to provide the best possible learning resources for Zendesk's customers. Anton started in technology with Microsoft as a visual designer and quickly moved into product development and technical communication. After Microsoft, he worked in various writing, product, user experience, and leadership roles at a software startup, a global e-learning company, Peoplesoft, Oracle, and Adobe.

Anton currently lives in Oakland, California, with his wife, Laura, and his dog, Siena. Anton is also an accomplished photographer specializing in portraits. He also enjoys traveling and music.

Colophon

The animal on the cover of *Practical Zendesk Administration* is a European nightjar (*Caprimulgus europaeus*). The Latin name refers to the old myth that these birds would suckle from goats at night, causing the goats to stop producing milk or even go blind.

This belief may have arisen from the fact that the birds were present around barns where insects were attracted to the farm animals. The concept of the goat-suckling nightjar was familiar even to Aristotle, though it does not appear in any Arab, Chinese, or Hindu traditions.

Nightjars are insectivores and do all of their eating on the wing. They hunt by sight and have relatively large eyes for birds their size; their eyes even have special reflective layers that improve night vision. Drinking and bathing also take place mid-flight after the bird makes a quick plunge into water to wash. Nightjars have unique serrated edges on their middle claws, which are used to preen and remove parasites.

Although European Nightjars are small, growing up to 11 inches from beak to tail, they can be quite effective hunters. They have been known to mob owls and other predators, and males will aggressively defend and protect their territories. Usually, a male will announce his presence with a long, 10 minute call that may change depending on where in his territory he is perched.

European nightjars spend the summer breeding in Western Europe and parts of Russia. They then migrate to sub-Saharan Africa for the winter, going as far as South Africa. They prefer a dry habitat of open country with trees and bushes for cover, but they do not build a nest. Instead, females roost on the open ground and protect their eggs by staying with them while the male patrols the boundaries of their breeding area.

Although European Nightjars are in danger from large predators like hawks, foxes, snakes, domestic dogs, hedgehogs, and weasels, the biggest threat to the world's nightjar population is habitat destruction. Additionally, the use of pesticides in Europe has greatly reduced the insect population upon which the nightjars feed.

The cover image is from Lydekker's *Royal Natural History, Vol. 4*. The cover fonts are URW Typewriter and Guardian Sans. The text font is Adobe Minion Pro; the heading font is Adobe Myriad Condensed; and the code font is Dalton Maag's Ubuntu Mono.

Get even more for your money.

Join the O'Reilly Community, and register the O'Reilly books you own. It's free, and you'll get:

- $4.99 ebook upgrade offer
- 40% upgrade offer on O'Reilly print books
- Membership discounts on books and events
- Free lifetime updates to ebooks and videos
- Multiple ebook formats, DRM FREE
- Participation in the O'Reilly community
- Newsletters
- Account management
- 100% Satisfaction Guarantee

Signing up is easy:

1. Go to: oreilly.com/go/register
2. Create an O'Reilly login.
3. Provide your address.
4. Register your books.

Note: English-language books only

To order books online:
oreilly.com/store

For questions about products or an order:
orders@oreilly.com

To sign up to get topic-specific email announcements and/or news about upcoming books, conferences, special offers, and new technologies:
elists@oreilly.com

For technical questions about book content:
booktech@oreilly.com

To submit new book proposals to our editors:
proposals@oreilly.com

O'Reilly books are available in multiple DRM-free ebook formats. For more information:
oreilly.com/ebooks

Have it your way.

9 781491 900697